As one of the world's longest established and best-known travel brands, Thomas Cook are the experts in travel.

For more than 135 years our guidebooks have unlocked the secrets of destinations around the world, sharing with travellers a wealth of experience and a passion for travel.

Rely on Thomas Cook as your travelling companion on your next trip and benefit from our unique heritage.

Thomas Cook **traveller** guides

SICILY
Martin Hastings

Your travelling companion since 1873

Written by Martin Hastings, updated by Elaine Trigiani
Original photography by Caroline Jones

Published by Thomas Cook Publishing
A division of Thomas Cook Tour Operations Limited
Company registration no. 3772199 England
The Thomas Cook Business Park, Unit 9, Coningsby Road,
Peterborough PE3 8SB, United Kingdom
Email: books@thomascook.com, Tel: + 44 (0) 1733 416477
www.thomascookpublishing.com

Produced by Cambridge Publishing Management Limited
Burr Elm Court, Main Street, Caldecote CB23 7NU
www.cambridgepm.co.uk

ISBN: 978-1-84848-370-5

© 2005, 2007, 2009 Thomas Cook Publishing
This fourth edition © 2011
Text © Thomas Cook Publishing
Maps © Thomas Cook Publishing/PCGraphics (UK) Ltd

Series Editor: Karen Beaulah
Production/DTP: Steven Collins

Printed and bound in Spain by GraphyCems

Cover photography © Saffo Alessandro/SIME-4Corners Images

Contents

Introduction

'Without Sicily, Italy leaves no image in the soul. Sicily is the key to everything…' *Johann Wolfgang Goethe*

One could say that Sicily is like Italy, only more so. All the characteristics of the Italian people, all the landscapes, archaeology, cuisine and history; they are all here in Sicily, but in a stronger and more dramatic guise.

Many visitors come to Sicily for the history, architecture and classical ruins. Once a colony of Greece, it grew so powerful that some of its classical architecture is more spectacular than that of Greece itself. Sicily is important for an understanding of southern Europe. Its strategic position in the middle of vital trading routes between East and West made it a vital military linchpin for controlling the whole of the Mediterranean. It is therefore not surprising to learn that every empire since the dawn of time has marched through Sicily, exploiting the island's riches and leaving vestiges of their passing: Phoenicians, Greeks, Romans, Saracens, Normans, French and Spanish.

A long history of foreign dominion may explain Sicilians' cautious attitude towards outsiders; however, despite this, Sicilians are on the whole courteous, welcoming and friendly, and have begun to realise that their island has cultural and natural gems that can

attract tourists from all over the world. Despite its surface flaws, which are all too sympathetically human – chaotic driving, crazy parking and disorganised town planning – Sicily is thick with charm and wonder.

Sicily is still wild; it is just being tamed. The rough edges have begun to be smoothed out, but real life still exists here, and in full force at that. Over and above the classical ruins and natural beauty, if you are sensitive to the opportunity, moving through Sicily is a chance to experience another culture. Get an insight into a culture being held from the brink of extinction by noticing how the forms of bread change from one area to another, which fishing methods are employed, and the variety of architectural solutions – from the humblest downspout to the utilitarian yet noble farm complexes of the *baglio* in the west and the *masseria* in the east.

Layers of history and culture are palpable too in the flavours of the gastronomy of the island and they can be tasted in wines as well as in traditional recipes. Traditional recipes mean not only those repeated lovingly by succeeding generations, but include those where the flavours of the past are re-elaborated intelligently by artisans with a strong sense of the island's history so as to assist in their continuing evolution, readying them for their journey into the future. This is another layer of the beauty of Sicily: there are sensitive craftsmen working with food, art and music who are all too aware of the impending danger of losing the cultural traditions of their region, and so work towards saving them and contributing to their continuing evolution.

While many visitors try to pack in as much as possible on their itinerary, it is also a pleasure to enjoy the island at a more sedate pace. The stunning natural wonders, such as Mount Etna, the Aeolian Islands or the lush forests in the north, cannot be rushed. The countryside tells you just as much about Sicily as the cities and other man-made cultural attractions. The luxuries of fine historic hotels and modern beach resorts are a treat, but so is a home-cooked meal at a family-run trattoria. In a land of contrasts, be sure not to miss out by narrowing your expectations.

Wild flowers in the Corleonese

The land

Sicily is the largest island in the Mediterranean, and the largest region in Italy, at 25,700sq km (9,926sq miles). Its volcanic soil is very fertile, and supports a rich variety of agricultural produce, vegetation and forests.

The island is mostly hilly or mountainous, with flat plains making up only a small proportion of the land area. The mountainous areas that dominate the island include many volcanoes, including the largest active volcano in Europe, and the highest point on the island, Mount Etna, at *c.* 3,300m (10,827ft). It is thought that the island might once have been part of the Italian mainland, with the northeast tip being only 3km (less than 2 miles) away from Calabria at the Strait of Messina, and just 160km (100 miles) from the African coast. Some argue that Sicily is slowly getting closer to Italy.

There are a large number of islands dotted around Sicily's shores, including the Aeolian Islands off the northeast, the Egadi Islands to the west and the Pelagie Islands off the southwest coast. All these are popular as resorts with good beaches, especially the biggest, the Aeolian Islands, which are famed for their volcanic black sands.

Sicily rests on two continental plates, which explains the area's reputation as a centre for seismic activity. The most recent major earthquake was in 1968 in the Belice valley where five towns were levelled; earlier, in 1908, the city of Messina was destroyed. Sicily is renowned for its volcanic instability. The most recent devastating eruption from Mount Etna occurred in 1669. It destroyed the city of Catania, with lava even reaching the sea. Etna is still very active and there were major eruptions in 2007, 2008 and 2010. Of Sicily's two other active volcanoes – Stromboli and Vulcano in the Aeolian Islands – only Stromboli regularly erupts with sparks and lava, its fireworks best seen by night.

Sicily's population is mostly settled on the coastal plains, while the mountainous interior is less populated. The main mountain ranges are the Nebrodi and Madonie, both in the north of the island, which are now protected as national parks.

Flora

The cultivation of the island throughout its long history, especially in Roman times, has had an impact on the geography of Sicily. Deforestation has slowed down in recent times, with some areas now nature reserves. There is a wide range of vegetation, much of it typically Mediterranean. There are many vineyards and olive groves, producing some of the finest wines, oil and olives in Europe. Orchards of almonds and pistachios are prevalent in the southeast and on Mount Etna. Citrus fruits and grain are widely cultivated, as are vegetables and other fruits, which are grown in quantity in greenhouses along the southern coasts.

Fauna

Fauna is not widely seen beyond the confines of the nature reserves, mainly due to the dense population and deforestation. Most commonly seen are sheep, and coastal birds such as seagulls and cormorants. Sicily's only poisonous snake can be found in the south, so care should be taken when visiting archaeological sites there. The Mount Etna region is home to some wild cats, rabbits and foxes. Other animals found on the island include the Sardinian wild boar and the Sardinian deer, well known in Orleans Park, Palermo. Tuna used to thrive off the coasts, but tuna schools have been decimated over the years, mostly by Japanese trawlers.

The land

The land

The environment

Despite the dramatic beauty of the island, which boasts some of the best scenery in Europe, this legacy has been tarnished by a poor environmental record. The fact that the Ministry for the Environment was only created in 1986 underlines the fact that environmental concerns have only recently been given much attention. Recycling is a new idea, but programmes are being instituted even in the interior.

Sicilian authorities have designated around 45 nature reserves, the first of which, Lo Zingaro, owes its creation to the success of a grass-roots movement. Regional parks were created in the mountainous woodland area of the Madonie and Nebrodi mountains. The Parco Naturale dell'Etna was created to stop development on the slopes of the volcano. Sicily is strong in the renewable energy sector, with a steady increase in wind farms and in the exploitation of solar power: at the Archimede Plant, opened in July 2010, the sun's heat is stored in molten salts to generate power when sunlight is lacking.

Industrialisation and urbanisation have created pollution, especially in cities and along the coastline. Illegal construction of buildings, mostly Mafia-funded, is also a problem. These *case abusive* (unauthorised houses) are built without permits and finished before the authorities can catch up with the perpetrators. The area around the Valley of the Temples near Agrigento was an eyesore until the government started demolishing the illegal houses there. In the interior of the island, there are many half-built houses. These avoid the taxes on 'finished' houses, and show

A dragonfly in Palermo's Orto Botanico

how poor the inhabitants of many rural communities are.

The economy

Agriculture dominates the island's economy: in particular, wheat and cereal grains, grapes, wine, olives, olive oil, almonds and citrus fruits. As the pillar of the economy, falling produce prices across the board and the rampant indebtedness of farmers give an indication of the state of the economy in general.

The island has a huge petrochemical industry and, surprisingly, in the 20th century, Sicily was ranked second only to the United States in sulphur production.

Despite its fertile soil and seas, the island is among the poorest regions in Italy. Unemployment is above 20 per cent and wages are a little more than half the national average.

Sicily's main industries have suffered at the hands of foreign competition and from lack of progress. The sulphur industry could not compete on the world market because of primitive extraction and transport methods. Much of Europe's tinned tuna, once provided by Sicilian fishermen, is now caught by more efficient Japanese vessels. Exports of citrus fruits have plummeted as foreign competitors have taken over the market.

Sicily's economy has endured huge problems throughout most of its modern history. Millions of lire (and now euros) have been poured into the

The rugged coastline at Isola Bella near Taormina

island in the form of development funds, but much of this – and of the money generated on the island since World War II – has been lost to the Mafia or to corrupt officials (basically the same thing). In the last decade, much European Union money has been spent on the island's infrastructure, especially roads and motorways and a controversial proposed bridge connecting Sicily to the mainland.

A bright spot is the waning of the immigrant mentality as the younger generations have adopted an entrepreneurial spirit, choosing to remain in Sicily or return after university to start their own businesses.

History

Sicily's geographical position in the heart of the Mediterranean has essentially dictated its history for 6,000 years. Its strategic importance both commercially and militarily has meant that it has been the target of colonisers and settlers, who have left a huge cultural legacy but who have also exploited the riches of the island. This goes some way to explaining the strong feelings of suspicion and insularity held by Sicilians towards outside governments, even the Italian authorities.

Although evidence of human settlers in Sicily dates from 12,000 BC, the first people known to have lived on the island, around 2000 BC, were three tribes: the Sicels from the Italian mainland, the Sicani from North Africa and the Elimi from Anatolia, legendarily Aeneas and his compatriots who landed on Sicily after fleeing burning Troy. The Phoenicians established trading posts at Palermo, Mozia and Solunto. Trade routes were already well established, and the island was growing prosperous by 734 BC when the first Greek colony was established at Naxos.

Magna Graecia

Beginning in the 8th century BC, land-starved Greek city-states began founding colonies on the Italian mainland and, from the 730s BC, on fertile Sicily. Prospering, they in turn founded sub-colonies so that the Greek-influenced area outside Greece itself came to be known as Magna Graecia, or Greater Greece. The colonies fought perennial border wars among themselves but formed strategic alliances when advantageous, as in 480 BC when Gela, Akragas and Siracusa together defeated the Carthaginians at Himera. With the Carthaginians held at bay, Siracusa ascended to primacy, eventually provoking the wrath of Athens itself, which in 415 BC sent the infamous Great Expedition to squash the upstart colony, only to suffer humiliating defeat. Internal clashes continued throughout Sicily as did attacks from Carthage, but Siracusa retained its status until making the fatal error of forming an alliance with Carthage in the Second Punic War.

Under Roman rule

The Punic Wars (Carthage versus Rome for control of the Mediterranean) were largely fought in Sicily. During the Second Punic War, in 211 BC, Rome sacked Siracusa, effectively bringing all of Sicily into its empire. Although the quaestors and praetors sent to rule

Sicily tended to pillage artistic treasures, the Roman period was relatively calm. *Latifondia*, large wheat-growing estates, were established and grain exports grew to such an extent that the island became known as the 'breadbasket' of the empire. Visible remains of the Roman age include the magnificent mosaics at the Villa del Casale and the systematic adaptation of Greek theatres to suit the Romans' more bloodthirsty tastes.

The Arabs

After the fall of the Roman Empire in AD 440, the Vandals briefly occupied the island, followed by the Byzantines in AD 535. However, it was the Arabs who next conquered Sicily, invading at Marsala in 827 and capturing Siracusa 50 years later. Occupation by the Saracens benefited the island greatly, with the introduction of new methods of agriculture and fishing, an expert system of irrigation and a better system of taxation. As the capital, Palermo became one of the most splendid cities in the Arabic world, on a par with Cordoba and Cairo.

The Normans and the Swabians

By 1040, the Normans were expanding across southern Europe, and eventually turned their eye to Sicily. The Norman conquest of Sicily took 20 years, but Palermo finally fell in 1071. Under the pragmatic rule of Roger I, Arab culture was assimilated. The island was Latinised, with French becoming the official language and Christianity the official religion. The first legal code was created, and patronage of the arts flourished under Roger's son, Roger II. His death in 1154 opened the door to 'William the Bad', with predictably bad results. However, his son, William II, built Monreale Cathedral, perhaps the greatest artistic legacy of the era.

As Holy Roman Emperors, the southern German Hohenstaufens, or Swabians, gained control of Sicily in 1194 when Frederick I Barbarossa's son, Henry VI, married Constance, daughter of Roger II. Their son, the enlightened Frederick II, ruled peacefully from his court in Palermo. It was during his reign that Sicily was westernised, losing most of its exotic influences.

French interlude

Desire for control of Sicily was fierce, and Frederick II's three heirs were killed so that, upon his death, the papacy was able to install Charles of Anjou as King of Sicily; he held court from Naples, marking the end for Sicily

Evidence of the Greeks at Siracusa

of a resident monarch. French rule was so hated that a popular revolt, the Sicilian Vespers, broke out in 1282, opening the door for an invasion by Peter of Aragon. When peace came in 1302, the Aragonese were firmly in control, and remained so for 500 years.

Spanish rule

Under the Spanish Inquisition and the powerful landed Sicilian nobility, starvation and poverty were a way of life for the rural population. Sicily slipped into decline: the Renaissance came and went without taking root on the island. By the end of the 15th century, Spain had discovered the Americas and was no longer interested in the affairs of Sicily.

Reforms did not go far enough to ensure that the lot of ordinary Sicilians improved much, and powerful land managers collected ground rents on behalf of absent landowners. This feudal system bred discontent, which gave way to sporadic uprisings by gangs of armed peasants who robbed from the large estates. Over the next era, these brigands became known as 'Mafia'.

During the 17th century, the fortunes of Sicily declined further. Etna erupted in 1669 devastating the east coast, and a huge earthquake in 1693 wiped out most of the cities in the southeast. Plague and cholera were rife. Revolts against the Spanish were brutally repressed. Under various treaties, Sicily was handed around, going in 1713 to the House of Savoy, and then to Austria. In 1735, it went back to Bourbon Spain. Sicily's revolutionary spirit fell short of that of late 18th-century France, and the island's aristocracy maintained its privileged position through repression of the peasantry.

During the Napoleonic Wars, the British attempted reform, forcing King Ferdinand to draw up a constitution in 1812, only for Ferdinand to annul it

Fallen telamon, originally part of the Greek Temple of Zeus, Agrigento

once Napoleon was defeated. Uprisings around the island culminated in a new provisional government by 1848, but it was Garibaldi's landing in Marsala in 1860 that swept away the tottering Bourbon state. He captured the island with peasant help later that year.

Dashed hopes for reform

The peasants' hope for land reform was dashed as Sicily was incorporated into the Piedmontese House of Savoy. Feudalism was abolished, but the real beneficiaries were not the ordinary peasants, but the bailiffs, who leased land from the owners and charged high rents, using local gangs to regulate affairs. These 'mafiosi' became intermediaries, filling the vacuum between the foreign government, ignorant of Sicilian affairs, and the people.

By 1894, a growing trade-union movement known as Fasci had been repressed, and mild reforms were discarded by the ruling gentry. The lack of land reform led to a growing wealth gap between the north of Italy and the impoverished south, particularly Sicily, sparking mass emigration.

The Messina earthquake of 1908 killed more than 80,000 people, further encouraging Sicilians to emigrate. When Benito Mussolini gained power over Italy in 1925, he was determined to crush the Mafia in Sicily. He was assisted in this aim by the landed gentry and their reward was the reversal of agrarian reforms, which returned the peasants once again to abject feudalism.

Mosaic detail in Monreale Cathedral

The modern era

The island endured further suffering during World War II, especially during Allied bombing raids. In 1943, the Allies invaded Sicily and, with the Mafia's help, were able to take it within 39 days. As a result, the Mafia tightened its grip on the island and helped the ruling classes to suppress left-wing movements after the war.

Communism was seen as a threat by the Church, and its political party, the Democrazia Cristiana (DC: Christian Democrats), grew in influence to become the most powerful Sicilian political force in the second half of the 20th century. It relied on the Mafia for election wins and, in return, Mafia business dealings were left alone. Campaigns against the Mafia have not stamped out political patronage, mismanagement and misappropriation of resources, although the Mafia's grip on business and government is much reduced (*see pp20–21*).

Sicily's architectural heritage

Most of Sicily's man-made wonders are remnants from the island's extensive colonial past, with some buildings being altered by successive rulers, from the Greeks, Romans and Arabs to the Normans and Spanish.

Greeks and Romans
Sicily was one of the great colonies of Greece, and in fact became a rival to its parent empire. One of the examples of this rivalry was demonstrated in the scale and innovation of Sicilian temples, which

A view of the cloisters at Monreale Cathedral

succeeded in outshining those in Greece itself. Remnants of these glorious years from the 8th century BC can be seen in the Valley of the Temples near Agrigento, at Selinunte and Segesta, and in the Neapolis Archaeological Park in Siracusa.

The Romans were not so creative, but tended to adapt existing Greek buildings for their own use. For example, Greek theatres such as the ones at Taormina and Siracusa were modified so that gladiatorial contests could be staged there. The most visited Roman ruins are the fantastically well-preserved mosaics at Villa Casale, near the town of Piazza Armerina. As well as enjoying the stunning craftsmanship of the mosaics, you can appreciate the layout of the villa complex, which shows the sophistication of Roman life.

Byzantines, Arabs and Normans
Assimilation and adaptation were the keynotes in the architecture of the Normans, and to a lesser extent the Byzantines and Saracens (Arabs). Greek temples were changed into Christian churches by the Byzantines, while the Saracens adapted them to become mosques. The Normans

then turned them back into churches. La Martorana and Chiesa San Giovanni degli Eremiti in Palermo are examples of this mixture of styles, the latter with Arabic red domes on the roof as well as Christian cloisters in the 'Arab-Norman' style. Another term applied to the architecture of the region is 'Sicilian Romanesque style', which describes the mix of Norman, Arabic and Byzantine influences in the same building.

The Capella Palatina in Palermo represents the height of Norman artistic achievement in Sicily. Under Roger II's enlightened rule, the chapel was built by craftsmen brought from all over Europe. There is exquisite Byzantine mosaic work covering most of the ceiling and walls, carved wooden panelling in the Arabic style, and superb Norman columns. The columns of Monreale Cathedral, another Norman masterpiece, are even more skilfully carved.

Of pure Arab parentage are contorted urban plans with hidden courtyards, antithesis to the grid pattern favoured by the Romans.

The decline of creativity

This kind of creativity ended with the arrival of the Hohenstaufen rulers in the 13th century. Like the Spanish after them, the emphasis was more on practicality and security than

artistic achievement. Perfectly illustrating this change of attitude was the use of the Greek theatre at Siracusa as a quarry: it provided stone to build the city's defensive walls. While the rest of Italy and Europe was experiencing the creative power of the Renaissance, Sicily, under Spanish rule, was unmarked by it.

The Baroque era

The next important period in Sicily's architecture began after the devastating earthquake of 1693 that hit eastern Sicily. Many towns like Catania, Noto and Ragusa were destroyed, needing almost total rebuilding. This gave the leading architects of the time the chance to build new cities from scratch. The top name in Baroque architecture at the time was Rosario Gagliardi. He pioneered a unique style that came to be known as Sicilian Baroque. The best examples of this are the churches of San Giorgio in Módica and Ragusa. Other exponents of the Baroque style were Andrea Palma, who designed the façade of Siracusa's cathedral, and Giovanni Vaccarini, the dominant force in the rebuilding of Catania.

The history of Sicily is reflected in its architecture. Some buildings incorporate many styles, such as the cathedrals in Palermo and Siracusa, and Palermo's Palazzo dei Normanni.

History timeline

12,000 BC	First known evidence of human settlers in Sicily.
1250 BC	First colonies founded by the Siculians, Elimians and Phoenicians.
735 BC	Naxian Greeks found Naxos, first colony on Sicily.
734 BC	Corinthians found Siracusa.
480 BC	Battle of Himera: Sicilian allies win a crucial battle against invaders from Carthage.
415 BC	Siracusa comprehensively defeats a massive Athenian fleet.
409 BC	The Carthaginians devastate Selinunte using unprecedented brutality.
212 BC	The Romans conquer Sicily; it is part of the empire for 200 years.
AD 827	Sicily is invaded by the Saracens and conquered by 902.
1032	Roger de Hauteville takes Palermo, beginning the Norman period.
1194–1266	The Hohenstaufens take control of the island.
1282	A popular revolt, the Sicilian Vespers, ousts the Angevins and opens the door to Spain.
1302	The Angevins and the Aragonese sign a peace treaty giving the Aragonese control.
1669	Mount Etna erupts. Ten villages are destroyed and lava reaches the sea at Catania.
1693	An earthquake destroys much of eastern Sicily, including Catania.
1720	Sicily passes to the Austrians.
1735	The Spanish reclaim Sicily under Charles I, a Bourbon.
1812	The Sicilian parliament ends the feudal system by introducing an English-style constitution.
1816	Ferdinand unifies Naples and Sicily, ruling as

Ferdinand I of the Two Sicilies.

1860	Garibaldi conquers the island and the Bourbons are expelled. The population votes for unification with Italy.
1880	Mass emigration to the USA begins via steamers from Palermo to New York and New Orleans.
1908	A huge earthquake strikes Messina, killing 100,000 people.
1930	Cesare Mori is sent by Mussolini to destroy the Mafia – and nearly succeeds.
1943	The Allies invade and take the island in 39 days.
1946	Sicily granted partial autonomy from Italy.
1968	Massive earthquake in the Belice Valley.
1972	Mafioso Tommaso Buscetta is arrested and cooperates with Italian judges, leading to many convictions.
1987	Over 300 Mafiosi convicted in Palermo Maxi Trials.
1992	Anti-Mafia judges Giovanni Falcone and Paolo Borsellino are assassinated.
1993	Toto Riina, Mafia boss in hiding, is arrested.
2001	Libera Terra begins producing agricultural products on land confiscated from the Mafia.
2003	Silvio Berlusconi, PM of Italy, is acquitted of laundering Mafia money.
2004	Two large-scale projects announced to boost the economy: a 520km- (323-mile) long gas pipeline to Libya and the Messina bridge to mainland Italy.
2006	Fugitive Mafia boss of bosses Bernardo Provenzano is arrested just before election day.
2008	Addiopizzo, an anti-Mafia business organisation, forms, indicating public revolt against the Mafia.
2010	Construction of the suspension bridge to the mainland is delayed by global economic crisis.

Politics

Sicily became an autonomous region within the Italian state in 1946. It is governed by the Assemblea Regionale Siciliana, the local parliament made up of 90 members. This is led by a regional president, whose Giunta (Cabinet) is made up of deputies who run the various government departments. There are nine provinces on the island; these take their name from their capital town, and they are known by their two-letter code (for example, Palermo province is PA).

Main political forces

The main forces in Sicilian politics over the last 50 years have been the Mafia and the DC (Democrazia Cristiana), the most influential party. They are said to have worked in collusion for most of this period. A series of corruption scandals throughout Italy in the 1990s uncovered the layers of institutionalised bribes and kickbacks, leading to the demise of the DC party. DC leader Giulio Andreotti was charged with Mafia association in 1993, but lived up to his reputation as a wily old fox by being sensationally acquitted in 1999. Nevertheless, the cosy relationship between the Mafia and political parties has mostly ended, but it remains to be seen whether Sicily can be governed without being controlled to a large extent by organised crime.

At the last regional election in April 2008, the main candidates were Raffaele Lombardo for a centre-right coalition (The People of Freedom, Movement for Autonomy, Union of Christian and Centre Democrats among them), which won with 65 per cent of the votes; and Anna Finocchiaro for centre-left (four parties), who received 30 per cent of the vote. The People of Freedom (*Il Popolo della libertà*) did secure 33 per cent of the vote, but there were 11 other parties.

Attitudes towards governance

Sicily's historical background of exploitation by foreign colonisers and land barons, coupled with the lack of social reform or equality throughout its history, has led to many Sicilians being understandably cynical about politics. In general, they see all politicians as corrupt and greedy, and therefore have little faith in government, which has been and is inextricably entwined with the Mafia. Indeed, the failure of government through most of the last two centuries to be in touch with – and improve the lot of – the ordinary citizen, has been one factor in the emergence of the Mafia. Originally, the

Mafia were the middlemen between absentee landlords and the ordinary islanders, helping to settle disputes.

With such high unemployment and precious little social security to fall back on, the Mafia was ironically seen as a relatively attractive provider of employment, security and welfare by the downtrodden.

With such an anti-establishment attitude, it is therefore no surprise that laws are seen as obstacles to be avoided, and road signs seen as merely 'an opinion'. The police do not seem to have a big influence in daily life, but are nevertheless very successful at looking good in their uniforms and shades, strolling around, drinking coffee and greeting their acquaintances.

Italy has been a unified country for less than 150 years, and there are difficulties in blending the political, social, economic and cultural differences of each region of Italy. Within Italy, Sicily is a very distinct region. In northern Italy, there is support for the idea that the country should be split into separate areas – north and south – and there are many in Sicily who agree with the idea. The Italian government is trying to level out the differences between north and south, particularly economic, and there are signs that Sicily is emerging from the poverty that has plagued it. It is difficult to dispute that Sicily is likely to be much better off, both politically and economically, within the bosom of a unified Italy.

A royal crest at the Palazzo Reale (also known as the Palazzo dei Normanni), Palermo

The Mafia

The public perception of Sicily was once dominated by the Mafia, shaped by films such as *The Godfather*, which accorded the members of this organisation almost mythical status. Misconceptions abound, so it is worth exploring the history of the Mafia in Sicily, in order to understand its influence on the island.

Beginnings

The Sicilian Mafia is said to have originated as a loosely organised community protection scheme during the French and Spanish occupations of Sicily. Locals formed their own law enforcement societies, rather than trusting corrupt foreign officials. It is suggested that the term is derived from the Arabic word *mu'afah* (place of refuge). *Mafiosi* was the name given to lawless brigands who attacked rich estates in the 13th century. In the 19th and early 20th centuries, Mafiosi existed only in the countryside, playing both sides by extracting rents for landowners from peasant farmers while at the same time offering 'protection' to the farmers.

The terms *cosa nostra* (this thing of ours) and *omertà* (the code of silence) arise from the ancient belief that problems should be taken care of without outside help or interference.

Mussolini and the war years

After Mussolini came to power in the 1920s, he gave Cesare Mori the task of destroying illegal organisations in Sicily. Mori sent troops into Sicily, utilising special powers to decimate the Mafia, imprisoning many and forcing others to flee to America.

During World War II, the Americans used Mafia connections in the USA – including 'Lucky' Luciano – to glean local knowledge of the island. This was invaluable during the invasion of Sicily in 1943, and ensured that Sicily was captured in just 39 days. Imprisoned mafiosi were set free, and the Mafia thrived as never before, coming to control most aspects of the island's life. Calogero Vizzini soon became *capo di tutti i capi* (boss of bosses) of the Sicilian Mafia. After Vizzini, a new breed of mafiosi emerged. They were more ruthless and willing to enter less 'respectable' arenas such as narcotics.

Riina and Buscetta

By 1968, a semi-literate farm-boy called Toto Riina had gained control of the Sicilian Mafia and wiped out the partnership of Mafia families on the island, the *Cupola*, much to the horror of traditional mafiosi. In 1980, one of its fleeing members, Tomaso Buscetta, went to Brazil to hide out from the brewing Mafia war. After a failed suicide attempt, he decided to break the code of silence and began his life as an informant. More than a dozen of his relatives were killed in revenge. Riina himself was arrested in 1993 and is currently serving numerous life sentences. However, Riina's arrest came too late to save the leading anti-Mafia judges Giovanni Falcone and Paolo Borsellini, whose assassination in 1992 sparked outrage and demonstrations throughout Italy.

The infamous Ucciardone Prison, Palermo, now home to many *mafiosi*

Recent developments

On 11 April 2006, Bernardo Provenzano, one of the most powerful Mafia bosses, was arrested. He had been a fugitive since 1963. Salvatore Lo Piccolo, another important boss, was arrested in 2007 and his son and potential successor was arrested in 2008. These arrests led many to think it was the beginning of the end for the Sicilian Mafia, while others saw the arrests as a political show involving marginalised members of the old Mafia, thereby assisting the new generation by allowing them to proceed under the radar.

The future

A potent sign of changing times is the very existence of groups such as Libera Terra and Addio Pizzo, anti-Mafia coalitions founded by courageous members of the community, which are continually gaining membership and influence.

However, many believe that the Mafia is far from dead. A new breed of 'white-collar' criminals has been described as *La Cosa Nuova* ('the new thing'). Nowadays, the Mafia is said to use legitimate businesses and government contracts, making it very difficult to measure success in the war against organised crime.

Culture

There is a rich cultural history on the island; Sicilians have produced world-renowned works in the fields of literature, art, music and theatre. For those with an interest in history, architecture and art, Sicily is a paradise. It is a veritable living museum of 10,000 years of Mediterranean art and architecture. Influences from Europe, North Africa and the East can be found across the island, as well as the work of local craftsmen, artists and architects, who preserve their own traditions.

Art

As early as the 7th century BC, Sicily became famous for art; here some of the best vase paintings of the Greek period were produced. From Roman times and the Middle Ages, the most famous works are the well-preserved mosaics at the Roman Villa in Casale near Piazza Armerina, and the marvellous Byzantine mosaics at Palermo, Cefalù and Monreale.

During the Renaissance, Sicily's greatest artist, Antonello da Messina (1430–79), emerged. His greatest works include *Portrait of an Unknown Man*, in the Cefalù Museo Mandralisca, *Polyptych of St Gregory*, in the Museo Regionale in Messina, the *Annunciation* in the Palazzo Bellomo in Siracusa and the *Virgin Annunciate* in Palermo's Palazzo Abatellis.

The most important painter from the second half of the millennium was Pietro Novelli, known as 'The Man from Monreale', who was prominent in the 17th century. In terms of modern painting, Renato Guttuso stands out in the 20th century. His 1950s depictions of modern living, produced in a colourful and vibrant style, are still relevant today, such as his paintings of La Vucciria market in Palermo. Just outside Palermo is the Galleria Comunale d'Arte Moderna e Contemporanea, in the town of Bagheria, where visitors can see the best examples of Guttuso's work, as well as his on-site tomb.

Literature

Throughout Sicily's history, great writers have emerged to produce classic works that remain famous to this day. Two of the earliest were the historian Diodorus Siculus, from the 1st century BC, and Theocritus from the 3rd century BC. Theocritus, from Siracusa, was famed for his pastoral poetry, which influenced many later writers.

By the 13th century, the first school of lyric poetry was developed at the court of Emperor Frederick II, and was known as the Sicilian School. The love poems of the school were written in Italian rather than Latin; its members are said to have invented the sonnet.

In literature, the 1800s saw the emergence of Giovanni Verga, who developed *verismo*, or the realistic novel. Luigi Pirandello dominated the first half of the 20th century; he won the Nobel Prize for Literature in 1934. He focused on the essential loneliness of humans and had a cynical view of life, describing the struggles of the lower classes. His works include *Il fu Mattia Pascal* (The Late Mattia Pascal), and *Sei personaggi in cerca d'autore* (Six Characters in Search of an Author). Salvatore Quasimodo was awarded the Nobel Prize for Literature in 1959 and

is well known for masterpieces of hermetic poetry such as *Ed è subito sera* (And Suddenly It's Evening).

One of the greatest of all Sicilian novels is *Il Gattopardo* (The Leopard), Giuseppe Tomasi di Lampedusa's only novel, published one year after his death, in 1958. It was translated worldwide and later made into the celebrated film by Luchino Visconti starring Burt Lancaster (*see pp54–5*).

Leonardo Sciascia (1921–89) is probably the most influential Sicilian writer of recent years; he highlighted injustices in Sicily such as corruption and social inequality. He was well known as an outspoken thinker and erstwhile politician. He wrote several crime-based novels, including *Il giorno della Civetta* (The Day of the Owl).

Buskers on the streets of Taormina

Music

Sicily's traditional folk music is much loved and today re-elaborated by performers like Nonó Salamone, Taberna Mylaensis, Guido Politi and his daughter, Matilde.

Of all Sicilian composers, Vincenzo Bellini is seen as the greatest. His most famous operas were *La Sonnambula* (The Sleepwalker), *I Puritani* (The Puritans) and *Norma*. He went against the fashion of composing seductive melodies and attempted to write music that was 'strongly felt and intimately wound up with the words'. His operas struggled for recognition until the revival of the *bel canto* style, and the acclaimed performance of Maria Callas in her 1953 title role in *Norma*.

Another well-known Sicilian composer is Alessandro Scarlatti (1659–1725), who was born in Palermo. He created a kind of lyrical opera in the 18th century that became known as the 'Neapolitan' style. Chief among his many works is the oratorio *Il Trionfo dell'Onore* (The Triumph of Honour).

Puppet theatre

The *opera dei pupi* (puppet theatre) is one of the most famous and popular forms of art of the Sicilian tradition and dates from the 1600s. The Normans are believed to have introduced this genre to the Sicilians, and it became hugely popular in the 1800s. Plays often represent the battles between Saracens and Christians in the Middle Ages. The chief characters are Orlando and Rinaldo, rivals for the hand of Angelica. The puppet theatre conveys ideals that are dear to Sicilian people: chivalry, honour, justice, faith, love. Other themes are social injustices; storylines often urge the downtrodden to rebel against the rich and powerful.

This form of theatre has been in decline for many decades, mostly due to the rise of cinema, television and the Internet, and many puppet theatres have closed. However, puppet shows remain a unique symbol in the Sicilian tradition and are popular with visitors to Sicily. The Museo Internazionale della Marionetta (International Puppet Museum) in Palermo has contributed greatly to preserving and supporting this art. There are puppet theatres in Palermo, Cefalù, Siracusa and Catania.

Theatre

A great deal is known about ancient theatre in Sicily, especially Greek theatre, as attested by the fascinating exhibits in Sicily's archaeological museums. The inventor of the Greek tragedy was Aeschylus, from the 5th century BC, whose works premiered in the famous Greek theatre in Siracusa. It wasn't until 1914 that Greek tragedies were once again performed in that theatre, and they are now staged regularly throughout the island.

There is also a rich tradition of theatre written and performed in the Sicilian dialect that spans from the

Middle Ages to the 19th century. One of the most important exponents of this was the playwright Nino Martoglio, who founded the Grande Compagnia Drammatica Siciliana (Great Sicilian Dramatic Society) in 1903.

Modern Sicilian theatre is dominated by Luigi Pirandello, who gained renown in the 1920s with his plays, *Enrico IV* (Henry IV) and an adaptation of *Sei personaggi in cerca d'autore*. The latter was seen as a challenge to the concept of stage representation.

A traditional puppet show, Palermo

Religion and festivals

Sicily's religious heritage is extremely varied, reflecting the theological influences of all the Mediterranean civilisations that have existed on the island. This variety can be seen in Sicily's range of temples, churches, mosques and other places of worship. There are a great number of festivals, both religious and secular – colourful, traditional celebrations of historical origin, festivals of the performing arts, as well as village food festivals.

Sicily is majority Roman Catholic and has been for 2,000 years. Most people still attend Mass once a week, and in general people are respectful of religious beliefs. Despite the Catholic veneer, pagan roots have not been lost. Talismans are worn to ward off evil spirits and if the evil eye has indeed been cast, it is not difficult to find someone with the power to lift it.

Many of today's religious festivals have roots in ancient pagan rituals. The chthonic fertility goddesses were worshipped throughout the Greek world and in Sicily in particular. Hence, fertility festivals dedicated to Demeter have morphed into popular sowing or harvest festivals, and are also linked to a convenient saint in the Roman Catholic pantheon. As an example, the grain harvest falls at the end of June as does the feast day of St Paul, and in Palazzolo Acreide, where the cult of the chthonic goddesses was strong, St Paul is celebrated with round loaves of bread (*cuddura*) harkening back to the round loaf baked in honour of Demeter.

Festivals
January
Epiphany (*La Befana*), *Piana degli Albanesi, near Palermo*. A parade and firework display.
February
Carnivale. Many towns stage carnivals during the week before Ash Wednesday. The festivities at Taormina and Sciacca are particularly well known.
Feast of St Agatha, *Catania*. The town's patron saint is celebrated with food, processions and fireworks (*3–5 February*).
March
St Joseph Suppers (*Cene di San Giuseppe*), *Santa Croce Camerina and the villages of the Belice Valley*. Preparation of local food for three personages representing the Virgin Mary, St Joseph and the Holy Child (*19 March*).
April
Easter (*Pasqua*). Holy Week is very important throughout Sicily, with

solemn processions and passion plays. Check out those in Trapani and Enna.

Gnocchi Festival, *Monterosso Almo.*

Motor Racing (*Corsa Automobilistica*), *Lago di Pergusa, near Enna (beginning of the racing season, last weekend of April).*

May

Tomato Festival (*Sagra del Pomodoro*), *Sampieri.*

June

Feast of St Paul, *Palazzolo Acreide (29 June).*

July

Feast of St Rosalia, *Palermo.* Palermo's patron saint is celebrated with partying, music and dancing (*11–15 July*).

August

Medieval Pageant (*Palio dei Normanni*), *Piazza Armerina.*

Notable food festivals include the **Onion Festival (*Sagra della Cipolla*)**, *Giarratana (15 August)*; the **Focaccia Festival**, *Chiaramonte Gulfi*; and the **Fish Festival**, *Pozzallo.*

September

Pilgrimages (*Pelegrinaggi*) are staged throughout Sicily. The most important are at Mount Pellegrino near Palermo (*4 September*) and at Gibilmanna in the Madonie (*8 September*).

Grape Festival, *Pedalino, hamlet of Comiso.*

Religion and festivals

The Feast of St Paul in Palazzolo Acreide

Impressions

Sicily is an outstandingly beautiful country; it comprises breathtaking volcanoes, dramatic mountains and islands; fantastic museums, churches and ancient sites – all illustrating gloriously the history of the Mediterranean; crystalline waters and beaches ideal for both sunbathing and scuba diving; and a sunny, dry climate that makes the holiday season last for eight months of the year.

What to see and do

The advantage of Sicily is the sheer variety of things to see and do. For example, there are stunning archaeological sites from Greek and Roman times, and from earlier civilisations, which could fill a whole month of sightseeing. The island's important strategic position in the Mediterranean has meant that successive colonisers have fought over Sicily throughout its history. Greeks, Carthaginians, Romans, Arabs, Normans, French and Spanish have all left their mark on the region's architecture, cuisine, customs, art and – of course – the people.

In terms of sightseeing, it is well worth staying in Palermo for at least a couple of days to visit the cultural sights. The ruins that really deserve to be seen, even if you are not an ancient history fan, are those at the Valley of the Temples in Agrigento, Segesta and Selinunte in the west of the island; the mosaics at the Roman villa at Casale in the centre of Sicily; and, of course, the Greek and Roman ruins that lie in and around the cities of Taormina and Siracusa on the eastern coast. Many of these sites have top-notch archaeological museums containing incredibly well-preserved artefacts from as early as 1500 BC.

It would be fair to say that each area of Sicily has plenty to offer a traveller: from ancient ruins to medieval villages, from natural beauty to cultural monuments, not forgetting the gastronomy and beaches. A visit to Mount Etna is also a must, not only for its beauty, but also to see the forces of nature at work first hand. There are many ways – to suit all levels of interest and fitness – to get up close to the volcano.

For astonishing scenery, look no further than the Aeolian Islands, a group of small islands with still-live volcanoes, black sandy beaches, superb diving and a very relaxing atmosphere. The weather can be hot, even outside

of the peak summer months, so the islands are well worth visiting at most times of the year.

For those who cannot get as far as the islands, there are lovely beaches along the entire circumference of Sicily, while the coast between Castellammare del Golfo and San Vito lo Capo is superbly picturesque.

For further exploration outside of the cities, Sicily has its fair share of nature reserves, ideal for hiking. The large area around Mount Etna is a big draw for nature-lovers. The Madonie Nature Reserve, not far from Palermo, and the Nebrodi Mountains, which lie just further east, both offer beautiful mountain scenery, picturesque villages and great walking, as does the Zingaro Nature Reserve near San Vito lo Capo.

Suggested itineraries

For those with limited time, a week in Sicily will give you a brief taste of the highlights of the island. As Sicily is the biggest region in Italy, it will involve a lot of travelling, so for some, doing this on an organised tour is a practical

The temple of Juno at Agrigento

The crowded beach at Cefalù

option. While it is possible to organise tours when in Sicily, bear in mind that these operate mostly in the summer, and many tourists prefer to book them from home.

For independent travellers with just a week or so to spend in Sicily, one suggested itinerary might be a day or two in Palermo (including a visit to Monreale); a day in Cefalù, a charming medieval seaside town east of Palermo; and a full day to enjoy the Valley of the Temples just outside Agrigento. Take in a day trip to Erice – a picturesque hilltop village in the northwest – and the ruins of Segesta, and spend another day in ancient Selinunte and the beach nearby.

Those with two weeks to spare could also include the gems on the east coast, such as Taormina, Mount Etna and

Siracusa, plus the towns of the Noto Valley in the southeast corner of the island (in particular the town of Noto itself) which are now a UNESCO World Heritage Site, famed for their superb Baroque architecture. Taormina and Siracusa in particular are each deserving of a couple of days so they can be enjoyed at a leisurely pace. Alternatively, beach-lovers might want to forgo the charms of the cities for the sandy beaches and dramatic scenery of the Aeolian Islands.

Visitors staying for longer than two weeks will have the luxury of visiting all of the sites mentioned above at their leisure, as well as unearthing further interesting towns and sights.

Sicily boasts enough ruins to keep travellers occupied for a month, as well as a number of quaint medieval towns, spectacular countryside and the rich cultural traditions of the villages of the interior.

How to get around

Sicily is the largest island in the Mediterranean but it is fairly easy to get around. For example, going from Palermo in the northwest to Catania on the far east of the island will take about three hours by car and four hours by bus. This means that it is not difficult to take in at least some of the island's sights in a reasonably short time. Most tourist sites are easily accessible

Impressions

A flock of sheep near Cava d'Ispica, southeast Sicily

A view over Modica in the southeast of the island

by public transport, so independent travellers tend to make their own way there rather than booking day-tours, though this is another option.

Buses are a convenient way of getting around. They are quick, reliable and excellent value. While trains are reasonably priced, too, service is not as complete and some railway stations are located outside town centres.

Hiring a car is the most popular option for visitors, and gives you the freedom to visit less accessible villages, monuments and beaches. Traffic in the cities is heavy, with seemingly undisciplined driving and chaotic parking. Find the method to the madness; driving is more organic than you might be accustomed to but not impossible to decipher. Take advantage of the reasonably priced car parks with attendants.

When to go

The best months to visit Sicily are May, June, September and October. Temperatures soar to the high 30s and low 40s C (over 100°F) in July and August, tourist centres are choked with visitors from all over Europe and hotel prices are at their highest.

People and conduct

The Sicilian people are a mix of races – including Greek, North African, Spanish, French and mainland Italian – that has developed over 3,500 years of history. Most Sicilians speak Italian in public, and Sicilian at home. This dialect is a rich patois that includes influences from Arabic, Greek and Spanish.

Sicilians are very welcoming but not necessarily easy to get to know, due to a mixture of factors: their general mistrust of outsiders, social injustice and Mafia control. Sicily as a whole has not seen huge numbers of tourists, and often the inhabitants' curiosity is counterbalanced by a natural suspicion. However, Sicilians are generally regarded as resilient and resourceful, with a good sense of humour. They are also very helpful to those who need it, and can be very courteous. However, be warned that, as on the mainland, many staff in the service sector, such as in shops or tourist offices, can come across as uninterested or even rude.

Traditional values

The family is incredibly important to Sicilians, the centre of which is *la madre* (the mother). Young Sicilians, as in the rest of Italy, tend to stay at home until they marry, and many young people still go to church. Traditional values are being eroded by a more consumer-oriented society, though even the youths on the street seem to have strong family ties. Sunday is the most important day of the week in terms of the family. In general, locals tend to have a good work–life balance. The journalist Luigi Barzini once explained that 'a happy private life helps people to tolerate an appalling public life'.

Sicilians are a very proud people, who do not take kindly to discourtesy towards themselves or Sicily in general. This means that they are very hospitable and will go out of their way to tell visitors about their region. However, they may become taciturn if too many personal questions are asked. One subject that is not discussed, especially with outsiders, is the Mafia.

Appearance is important

Italian men openly appreciate female beauty, but they appreciate traditional southern Mediterranean discretion as well. Foreign females showing too much flesh are likely to be at least whistled at, if not fully propositioned. Despite the obsession with the female form – in advertising, TV and in the street – Sicilians are unaccustomed to and disapprove of skimpy clothes, and in general the attitude towards dress is traditional, particularly in the provinces. This is reflected in the way all ages are clothed. Men tend to wear trousers, even in the summer, and women do not wear very short skirts. Even youngsters dress in a similar style according to their peer group, which means that jeans and T-shirts predominate. Public appearance is seen as important, and you will often see families, dressed up smartly, enjoying their evening stroll. Beachwear is for the beach only.

General behaviour

Sicilians are scrupulously honest in their dealings with each other and visitors. It is almost unheard of to be short-changed in shops or bars, and most guesthouses are run efficiently and courteously. Tipping in restaurants is not compulsory, but a few euro left on the table is always appreciated.

Lifestyle

It is worthwhile adjusting to the Sicilian pace of life as soon as possible after you arrive on the island. It is slower than northern Europe, so it is best not to expect too much in terms of efficiency. Many visitors are dismayed at the chaotic traffic and haphazard parking in the streets, as well as the lack of queuing in cafés or at bus stops.

Remember that many museums and shops are closed between 1pm and 4pm. The best plan is to do lunch and then take a siesta or use that time for travel. On Sundays, especially outside the cities, many establishments are closed and public transport is reduced.

A Sicilian breakfast consists of an espresso coffee or cappuccino with a *cornetto* (croissant); or, at a café, a *granita* or *gelato* with a brioche (soft, sweet bun).

Locals tend to eat dinner late, so not many restaurants open before 7pm.

Entertainment in the evenings often consists of a *passeggiata* (evening stroll) around town. In many towns at the weekends, the streets and squares are filled with families taking in the cooler evening air and bumping into friends at every corner. There are surprisingly few bars and no drinking culture to speak of. Family life tends to dominate, although this tradition is gradually being eroded. Sicilians tend to dress smartly for dinner, with few wearing shorts or sandals, even in the summer.

Mafia and crime

Sicily's most famous modern painter, Renato Guttuso, gave his verdict on the island: 'In Sicily, you can find dramas, pastorals, idylls, politics, gastronomy, geography, history, literature…in the end you can find anything and everything, but you can't find truth.'

While the Mafia is a reality in Sicily, tourists are extremely unlikely to be aware of its presence even though it now owns many legitimate businesses, restaurants and hotels. There is relatively little crime against tourists, other than petty crime in Palermo and Catania, although visitors should take the usual precautions, especially at night. The situation has improved a great deal in the last 12 or so years, with the authorities cracking down on undesirable elements, particularly in Palermo.

If you prefer to avoid hotels and restaurants with Mafia ties, contact Addio Pizzo's travel agency (*www.addiopizzotravel.it*).

Café surroundings – here in Taormina – enhance a good breakfast

Palermo

'The past is never dead, it isn't even past.' William Faulkner's reflection on time is evident in Palermo. The city perfectly represents the island of Sicily with layers of history and culture, not buried one under the next, but blending seamlessly. The vibrations of modern reality add another dimension to the cultural richness of Palermo where one million inhabitants and their vehicles live within a space that grew organically from a Phoenician trading post and Moorish kasbah.

Palermo is undergoing a revival of sorts, with historic buildings being restored and street crime being tackled head on. The result is that more visitors are choosing to spend time in the city. The attractions of superb and varied architecture, important museums and churches, and a selection of fine restaurants and hotels, are proving a winning combination for ever-expanding tourist numbers.

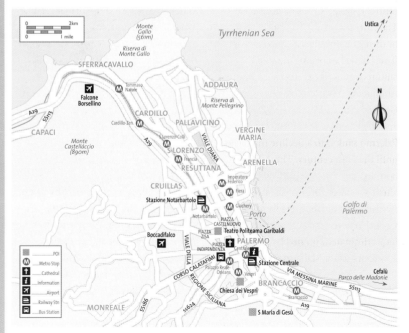

Background

The capital of Sicily was, in the Middle Ages, one of the great cities of Europe. Its conquest by all the major colonisers of the Mediterranean throughout its history has left it a huge legacy of architecture and art, something that the European Union is feverishly trying to protect. Built along a wide bay at the foot of Mount Pellegrino, Palermo has always been an important trading port.

The origins of the city go back to the 8th century BC when the Phoenicians established the first town here, called Ziz. The Greeks then called it Panormos (port). A small town under the Romans and Byzantines, it flourished under the Arabs as a cultural centre, rivalling Cordoba and Cairo. The Normans made Palermo the capital of their kingdom in 1072 under Roger I. It was hailed as one of the most cultured cities in 12th-century Europe. After being passed wholesale over to the German Hohenstaufens and Frederick I, and then to the French Anjou family, Palermo sank into a decline that lasted until the 20th century. The Allies bombed the city in World War II and, after the end of the war, the population swelled as rural labourers looked for work. However, the city was rebuilt indiscriminately, funded by corrupt city governors using Mafia money.

Planning a tour

Among the most important tourist attractions of Palermo are the Palazzo

Fontana Pretoria, Piazza Pretoria

dei Normanni with its Cappella Palatina (Palatine Chapel), a treasure of Arab-Norman architecture; La Martorana, a splendid Norman church with a notable mosaic cycle; the beautifully restored Teatro Massimo; and the dynamic Ballarò market. Key museums include the Galleria Regionale in Palazzo Abatellis, and the extensive Museo Archeologico Regionale, which displays Sicilian archaeological finds.

It is worth sampling some of the delicious pastries and desserts, as well as making the most of the many dining choices, especially around Piazza Castelnuovo and the Politeama Theatre. *Tourist information offices: Piazza Castelnuovo 34. Tel: (091) 605 8111. www.palermotourism.com. Open: Mon–Fri 8.30am–2pm & 2.30–6.30pm. Airport. Tel: (091) 59 1698. Open: Mon–Sat 8.30am–7.30pm.*

PALERMO'S HISTORIC CENTRE

The historic centre is divided into four *canti* (districts): La Kalsa, Albergheria, Il Capo and la Vucciria, which meet roughly at the Quattro Canti, a historic junction at the crossroads of Via Maqueda and Corso Vittorio Emanuele. This is a good reference point when exploring the city.

North of the Quattro Canti is the so-called 19th-century city, centred around Piazza Castelnuovo, which contains the more sophisticated shops, restaurants and hotels. South of Quattro Canti, towards the Stazione Centrale (central train station), lie most of the budget hotels and restaurants. Stazione Centrale lies at the southern end of the historic centre, and is another important reference point; most of the city buses leave from here. The two main avenues heading northwest from the station are Via Roma and Via Maqueda, which run past Quattro Canti towards the 19th-century part of the city.

At the western border of the historic city is Palazzo dei Normanni, an important monument, and to the east is the old, natural port of La Cala.

The historic centre of the city displays the many cultural influences that have shaped Sicily, as well as giving the visitor an authentic taste of Palermitan life. Most of the newest, chic restaurants, hotels and shops are in this area, as well as some of the most run-down and downright decrepit streets in the city. One cannot help being impressed by the vibrancy of the city and the pulsating fascination of the street life. The sheer number of historical buildings, churches, museums and cultural sights packed into the historical centre is remarkable.

Albergheria

This district extends slightly east beyond the Quattro Canti, to include the sights around Piazza Pretoria such as the churches of La Martorana and San Cataldo. It extends all the way to the western border of the historic centre, to Palazzo dei Normanni, one of the most important monuments in the city, and encompasses the Ballaró market.

Il Mercato di Ballarò

Of Palermo's three main markets the most dynamic is the Ballarò. The already teeming streets give way to overloaded tables and stands selling *ogni ben di dio* (every gift of God): all sorts of fresh produce and still-wriggling fish. Butchers' shops operate in the open air, and vendors lure potential customers shouting call-and-response boasts of what they've got to offer: '*Cerase bedde cerase bedde cerase beddeeeeee!*' And indeed the cherries are beautiful.

However, it's not all raw ingredients: Sicilian street food is some of the best in Italy and you can snack at stalls selling *arancini* (stuffed rice balls), *panelle* (chickpea-flour fritters), *pan conzatu* (a minimal sandwich, but the Sicilian ingredients make one a real treat) and *pani ca'meusa* (spleen sandwich, anyone?).

Piazza Ballarò, Piazza del Carmine and surrounding streets.

Palazzo dei Normanni (Royal Palace)

The Palazzo Reale, also known as the Norman Palace, is the seat of Sicily's regional government. The castle was originally a Roman fort that was built on by the Arabs in the 9th century before being expanded by the Normans in 1132. It is a suitably imposing location and was Roger II's seat of Sicilian administration in the 12th century. It also contained his harem.

The exterior is striking, but austere, whereas the interior has a majestic feel

to it, dating from the time when the Normans' Kingdom of Sicily was the most prosperous country in Europe.

On the first floor above the courtyard is the Capella Palatina (Palatine Chapel), which should not be missed on any visit to Sicily. It is the most stunning example of the Norman kingdom's wealth, and the height of Arab-Norman artistry. Built in 1132 during Roger II's reign, this basilica is decorated with stunning Byzantine mosaics of biblical scenes from both the Old and New Testaments. A highlight is the intricately carved wooden ceiling in the Arab stalactite style.

Piazza del Parlamento. Tel: (091) 705 1111. Open: Mon–Sat 8.15am–5.45pm

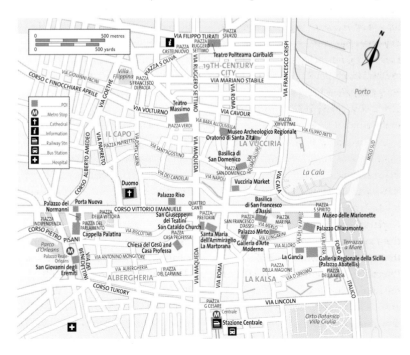

One of the striking façades overlooking the Quattro Canti

(last admission 5pm), Sun 8am–noon. Chapel closed Sun and holidays 9.45–11.15am. The Appartamenti Reale can be closed for parliamentary functions and the chapel for weddings; call ahead for information. Admission charge.

Piazza Pretoria

This square is dominated by the fountain and sculptures created by the Florentine sculptor Francesco Camiliani in 1555. The Fontana Pretoria caused a scandal when it was first unveiled, and was named 'the fountain of shame'. It is surprising that it was allowed to be erected at all, as it was constructed during the Spanish Inquisition.

The fountain was originally commissioned by Viceroy Don Pedro de Toledo for a palazzo in Florence, but his son sold it to the city authorities and the fountain was shipped to Palermo. Just in front of the fountain is the Municipio (City Hall), where protesters occasionally congregate.
Via Maqueda, just southeast of Quattro Canti.

Quattro Canti

The Quattro Canti is at the heart of historic Palermo, a busy intersection that is a convenient starting point from which to explore, since many of the city's sights can be reached from here on foot. The original name of this famous crossroads is Piazza Vigilena, named after the Spanish Viceroy who built it in 1611. Baroque sculptures of patron saints and Spanish royalty dominate the buildings on the four corners of the intersection, each made up of three storeys, which are the work of Giulio Lasso.
Located at the intersection of Corso Vittorio Emanuele and Via Maqueda.

San Cataldo church

This tiny church with its bulbous red domes is a splendid example of elegant Arab-Norman craftsmanship. Left unfinished, the unadorned interior is articulated by delicate tracery windows and intricate, inlaid marble floors. Next to La Martorana, it was constructed by Maio of Bari, who was the *emir* (first

minister) of King William I 'The Bad' in 1154. However, Maio was murdered six years later and it was never finished. This explains the lack of interior adornment. The remains of a Roman wall sit at the bottom of this site, down the steps, and to the side is a useful tourist information kiosk.
Piazza Bellini 2. Tel: (091) 616 1692. Open: daily 9.15am–1pm & 3.30–6.30pm. Admission charge.

San Giuseppe dei Teatini (St Joseph of the Theatines)

San Giuseppe dei Teatini is a great example of Baroque exuberance. The chapels are richly decorated with stucco and frescoes, and the high altar drips with semi-precious stone. The church was built by Giacomo Besio in 1612 and the dome was added in the 18th century. The façade is neoclassical and was designed in 1844.
Southeast corner of the Quattro Canti. Open: Mon–Sat 8.45–11.15am & 5–7pm, Sun 8.30am–1pm. Free admission.

Santa Maria dell'Ammiraglio (Saint Mary's of the Admiral)

More familiarly known as 'La Martorana', this is the most famous medieval church in the city. It was built in 1143 using funds donated by George of Antioch, admiral during the reign of King Roger II. Its nickname dates from 1433 when it was presented to a Benedictine order founded by Eloisa Martorana. The attractive bell tower is from the original Arab-Norman building. As with many Arab-Norman churches, some Baroque features and frescoes were later added,

San Cataldo Church, Palermo, with its red cupolas

and their flamboyant style sit uncomfortably with the more restrained Byzantine mosaics. This is the first mosaic cycle executed on the island and stunning for the masterful Byzantine craftsmanship. Note the mosaic in the narthex that shows Christ crowning King Roger II. Although merely audacious now, it was controversial at the time: it was regarded as a challenge to the Pope in that it depicts the king's authority being handed directly to him from God.

The church is often used for weddings and baptisms, in which case you may have to wait to go inside.

Piazza Bellini 3. Tel: (091) 616 1692. Open: daily 9.15am–1pm & 3.30–6.30pm. Admission charge.

Il Capo

Here to the southwest of Quattro Canti you'll find Palermo's cathedral and the new contemporary art museum (*see p43*), as well as markets and a warren of characterful alleyways.

Duomo (Cathedral)

The city's duomo is certainly imposing from the outside, and there is plenty of room in the square in front from which to appreciate the attractive exterior. The

The Catalan Gothic porch of Palermo's Duomo

exterior is a veritable mishmash of architectural styles that sometimes clashes rather than complements. It gives a fascinating picture of how Sicily has been shaped by the architecture of foreign invaders.

Officially known as Santa Maria Assunta (St Mary of the Assumption), a Byzantine Greek Orthodox church once stood here. This became a mosque when the Arabs conquered Palermo in 831. In 1072, it was reconsecrated as a Christian church. The cathedral has been greatly modified through the ages, so little of the original structure remains. Alterations in the 18th century gave the interior a neoclassical look.

The chapel nearest to the main entrance of the church contains the tomb of King Roger and other royal tombs. The Cathedral Treasury contains some fine religious objects, and the jewel-encrusted, 12th-century tiara of Constance of Aragon.

Corso Vittorio Emanuele. Tel: (091) 334 373. www.cattedrale.palermo.it. Open: daily 9am–5.30pm. Free to the cathedral; admission charge for entering the Treasury and Crypt.

Markets

At the flea market (*mercato dei pulci*), you'll find antique furniture, old chandeliers and recovered majolica tiles. The area's food market (*Mercato del Capo*) rivals the Ballarò for local colour.

Flea market. In and around piazzas Papireto and Domenico Peranni, just behind the Duomo.

Mercato del Capo. In and around Via Porta Carini.

Riso, Museo d'Arte Contemporanea della Sicilia (Museum of Contemporary Art of Sicily)

Palazzo Riso, a 19th-century construction that was home to the Barone Riso in the 20th century, is now the site of Palermo's museum of contemporary art. The permanent collection represents Sicily's contemporary art scene, happily on the rise of late. The active exhibitions programme focuses on national and international themes and artists. Ample didactic programmes are offered for all ages.

Corso Vittorio Emanuele 365. Tel: (091) 320 532. www.palazzoriso.it. Open: Tue, Wed, Sat & Sun 10am–8pm, Thur & Fri 10am–10pm. Admission charge.

ARCHITECTURAL FEATURES OF THE CATHEDRAL

The architectural hotchpotch of styles within the cathedral makes it a fascinating building to explore, and to identify the various elements that have been added through the years. Here are some things to look out for when you walk around the cathedral:

The Catalan Gothic Portico dates from 1430. Note the carved biblical scenes.

The slender towers are also Gothic, with double-lancet windows, added to the Norman clock tower in the 15th century.

The cupola is Baroque in style, added in the 18th century by Ferdinando Fuga.

The left-hand column of the southern portico includes inscriptions from the Qur'an.

Walk: The Càssaro

This walk focuses on the sights along the Corso Vittorio Emanuele, which connects the Palazzo dei Normanni and the sea. Also known as the Càssaro, this is the oldest street in Palermo and dates back to the Phoenician settlement. Either walk southwest from Quattro Canti on Corso Vittorio Emanuele, or take one of several orange city buses that travel the Corso (such as no 105).

Allow about three hours.

1 Palazzo Riso
(Museo d'Arte Contemporanea della Sicilia)
Visit Palermo's new Sicilian contemporary art museum to get an idea of how artists today are inspired by the rich, contrasting nature of Sicilian culture. Call or check their website for special exhibitions and didactic programmes.
Corso Vittorio Emanuele 365 (facing Piazza Bologna). Tel: (091) 320 532. www.palazoriso.it. Open: Tue, Wed, Sat & Sun 10am–8pm, Thur & Fri 10am–10pm. Outside, turn right and walk up the Corso until you reach the Cathedral.

2 Duomo
Its original Norman construction has been tinkered with over the centuries and the later Arab, Gothic and 18th-century influences have ruined its aesthetic cohesion. Take at look at the superb Treasury and Royal Tombs inside. Do not miss the exterior of the original Norman apse on the east side.

Outside, turn right, walking along the busy Corso Vittorio Emanuele. Cross the road to the park opposite.

3 Piazza della Vittoria
Although not as impressive as it must have been in its heyday, it is still worth strolling around this park, if only to avoid the traffic on the busy road. It was – in times gone by – the military, political and administrative heart of Sicily, and was also a venue for public festivities in the 17th and 18th centuries. *Continue walking along Corso Vittorio Emanuele to the Porta Nuova.*

4 Porta Nuova
Be watchful of the traffic as you walk through this massive gate with its májolica cupola and enormous, turbaned Hermes statues. For the past 400 years, it has served as a demarcation line between the old and new city. It was built in 1535 to commemorate the victory of Holy Roman Emperor Charles V over the Tunisians.

Beyond the gate, turn left, following the castle walls, past the bus stop opposite Piazza Indipendenza (where buses leave for Monreale), till you reach the gates of the palace on your left.

5 Palazzo dei Normanni

Now the seat of the regional government, this royal palace was built by the Arabs in the 9th century, extended by the Normans and restructured by the Hohenstaufens.

Tickets for the Capella Palatina and the Appartamenti Reali are available from the booth in front of the palace. Walk around the impressive courtyard before ascending to the chapel.

Dedicated to St Peter, this example of Arab-Norman artisanship is breathtaking in its beauty. Take time to appreciate the magnificent Byzantine mosaics, elaborately painted and carved wooden roof, and marbled lower walls and floor. When it gets busy, you may have to queue, as this relatively small chapel can get packed by tour groups, especially in the summer.

If you make your way back to Via Maqueda as the crow flies, the route will pass through some characterful residential streets. Some may prefer to backtrack to Piazza della Vittoria and Corso Vittorio Emanuele, especially if it is starting to get dark.

Walk: The Càssaro

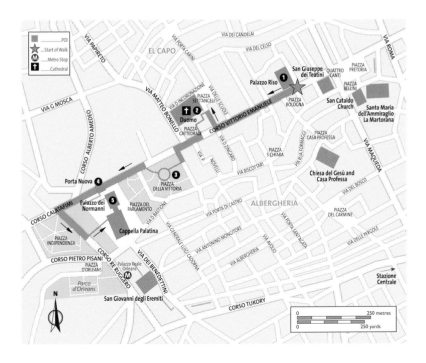

La Vucciria

This district used to be famed for its vibrant market, which has seen better days. The Sicilian artist Renato Guttuso (1911–87) immortalised the market in his vibrant 1974 painting *La Vucciria*, on view at Palazzo Chiaramonte. At first, the district appears just a maze of rundown alleys and dilapidated buildings, but exploring reveals artists' studios, good restaurants and bars. Sights include the important Museo Archeologico Regionale and the Basilica di San Domenico.

Basilica di San Domenico

Very near Vucciria market is this Baroque building, notable for the array of famous citizens buried here. The tombs and cenotaphs include Francesco Crispi, the first prime minister of a unified Italy. The square in front of the church is a chaotic piazza, used as a car park, and home to the obelisk Colonna

The Baroque grandeur of the Basilica di San Domenico

dell'Immacolata. The church was built in 1640 by Andrea Cirincione.

Behind the church is the 16th-century Oratorio del Rosario, with an Anthony Van Dyck altarpiece.
Piazza San Domenico, off Via Roma. Tel: (091) 584 872. Open: Tue–Fri 8.15am–12pm, Sat & Sun 5–7pm. Free admission.

Entrance to the Oratory is at 16 Via Bambinai. Open: Mon–Sat 9am–1pm. Free admission.

Museo Archeologico Regionale (Regional Archaeological Museum)

This impressive museum is housed in a splendid building that was a 17th-century monastery, and it boasts a very pleasant courtyard. The collection is one of the most important in Italy and contains items from the Phoenician, Punic, Greek, Roman and Saracen eras. Among the most valuable pieces are the Pietra di Palermo, a black slab with inscribed hieroglyphics dating from 2900 BC, and the *metopes* of Selinunte, stone-relief carvings recovered from the Greek temples of Selinunte. The building is undergoing renovation, hence some rooms are closed until 2012.
Via Bara all'Olivella 24. Tel: (091) 611 6805. Open: Tue–Sat 8.30am–1.30pm & 3–6.15pm, Sun 8.30am–1.30pm. Admission charge.

Oratorio di Santa Zita (Oratory of Santa Zita)

Behind San Domenico and past the Largo Cavaliere di Malta, visit this

Fruit seller at the famous Vucciria market

small oratory, every square inch of which was decorated by Giacomo Serpotta, master of buoyant stucco work. Putti (cherubs), garlands and colourful inlaid stone provide theatrical surrounds for depictions of vaious allegories, including a high relief of the 1571 naval Battle of Lepanto, which gave Spain and its allies control of the Mediterranean.
Via Valverde 3 (corner Via Squarcialupo). Open: Mon–Sat 9am–1pm.

La Kalsa

To the east of the Quattro Canti is this fascinating district, until recently a no-go area for visitors. It was settled by the Arabs and has been notorious since the Middle Ages for seedy characters and crime, even after its partial destruction in World War II. It is therefore ironic that its name derives from an Arabic word, *khalisa*, meaning 'pure'. The area is much improved, and visitors are discovering the many historic sights and new, chic bars, restaurants and hotels.

Basilica di San Francesco d'Assisi (Basilica of St Francis of Assisi)

The Basilica of St Francis of Assisi is an attractive medieval church that has undergone many changes since it was built in 1277. Once a Franciscan monastery, it has retained its medieval atmosphere, despite being destroyed by Frederick II when he was ex-communicated by the Pope. Ironically, it took the Allied bombing in World War II to persuade the restorers to remove the later modifications in an effort to return the church to its original appearance. Highlights include the exquisite rose window, the beautiful cloister and some fine sculptures by the Gagini family. Behind the high altar are wooden choir stalls dating from 1520.

Piazza San Francesco d'Assisi. Tel: (091) 616 2819. Open: Mon–Sat 7.30am–12pm & 4.30–5.30pm, Sun 4.30–5.30pm. Free admission.

Galleria d'Arte Moderna (Gallery of Modern Art)

Housed in a 15th-century Catalan-Gothic palace and the adjacent 17th-century former Franciscan convent, this gallery shows art from the 19th and 20th centuries by Italian artists such as Renato Guttuso, Emilio Greco and the famous Futurist painter Giorgio de Chirico.

Via Sant'Anna 21. Tel: (091) 843 1605. www.galleriadartemodernapalermo.it. Open: Tue–Sun 9.30am–6.30pm. Admission charge.

Galleria Regionale della Sicilia

Beautiful Gothic Palazzo Abatellis, commissioned as a private palace in 1488 by Palermo's harbour-master, now houses Sicily's regional art museum. Later used as a monastery, it is severely Gothic in style. It has a large, attractive courtyard. The post-war renovation by Carlo Scarpa is a notable work of modern Italian architecture.

Highlights of the collection are the stylised bust of Eleanor of Aragon, one of the greatest sculptures on the island, made by Francesco Laurana in 1471; Antonello da Messina's breakthrough oil paintings, *Our Lady of the Annunciation* and his group of three saints including St Jerome with delicate face and hands; the intricate *Malvagna Triptych* by the Flemish artist Mabuse; and the downright scary *Triumph of Death* fresco by an unknown 15th-century artist.

Via Alloro 4, at the seaward end beyond Piazza della Kalsa. Tel: (091) 623 0011.

Open: Tue–Sun 9am–12.30pm.
Admission charge.

Museo delle Marionette (Marionette Museum)

The Marionette Museum, dedicated to the art of puppetry, is one of the most important of its kind in the world. Puppetry has been an important part of traditional Sicilian entertainment since Norman times. Each region of the island has its own puppet styles, especially those in Catania and Palermo, mostly centred around tales of Norman Sicily, with chivalrous heroes, Arab pirates, princesses and troubadours. There is a large international collection of puppets, too, from as far afield as Vietnam, India and Indonesia.

From October until 15 June, the museum puts on free puppet shows, while in summer, puppet shows are performed at Teatro Argento.
Piazzetta Niscema 1. Tel: (091) 328 060.
Open: Mon–Sat 9am–1pm &
2.30–6.30pm, Sun 10am–12pm.
Admission charge.
Teatro Argento. Corso Vittorio Emanuele
445. Tel: (091) 611 3680.
Shows daily 5.30pm. Admission charge.

Palazzo Mirto

This 19th-century nobleman's mansion is an absolute jewel, because the original furnishings have been miraculously retained to the present day. The palazzo was built in the 18th century and owned by aristocratic families, the last of which was the Filangeri family, who donated it to the nation in 1982. The sheer luxury of the décor and furnishings is extraordinary. The best drawing rooms include the Sala degli Arazzi (Tapestry Hall) with mythologically themed paintings by Giuseppe Velasco. Also worth looking out for is the courtyard, which boasts an excessively ornate Rococo fountain.
Via Merlo 2, off Piazza Marina.
Tel: (091) 616 4751. Open: daily
9am–7pm. Admission charge.

The lavish Palazzo Mirto

Walk: Around Piazza Marina, La Kalsa

This walk in La Kalsa district takes in the main sights of this gritty but stimulating neighbourhood.

Allow three hours (depending on the amount of time spent in the galleries).

1 Piazza Marina

This used to be the main square in Old Palermo, used from the Middle Ages onwards for public executions, knights' tournaments and theatre performances. It was once part of the harbour, but this area has long since silted up and been reclaimed. Its central garden, the Giardino Garibaldi, is shaded by fig and banyan trees.

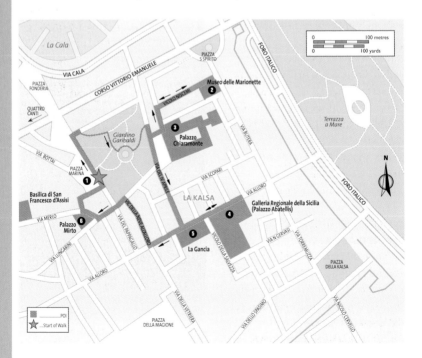

From the east side of the gardens, walk up the steps, go right and left into the lane leading to Vicolo Niscemi.

2 Museo delle Marionette

This is one of the most important puppet collections in the world, with more than 2,000 marionettes. It gives a fascinating insight into this originally Norman tradition, now very much part of Sicilian cultural history.
From the museum, retrace your steps, turn left and walk 50m (55yds) to find Palazzo Chiaramonte on the left.

3 Palazzo Chiaramonte, or Steri

This palace was built in the early 1300s as a residence for powerful Manfredi Chiaramonte, Count of Modica, in a style midway between medieval fort and patrician palace that became known as the Chiaramonte style. Formerly the seat of the Sicilian Inquisition, it now houses the offices of the university. Guided tours include Inquisition-era frescoes, medieval painting and Renato Guttoso's famed *Vucciria*.
Piazza Marina 61. Open: Tue–Sat 9am–1pm & 2.30–6.30pm, Sun 10am–2pm. Admission charge.

4 Galleria Regionale di Sicilia (Palazzo Abatellis)

This splendid Catalan Gothic building was built in the late 15th century for Francesco Abatellis. The large courtyard leads into the impressive collection of the Regional Gallery.
Go left to the 15th-century church.

5 La Gancia

The formal name for this church, built in the 1490s, is the Chiesa di Santa Maria degli Angeli. It houses Palermo's oldest organ (1620), which is located above the main doorway. The interior is known for its decorative modern ceiling and beautifully carved pulpit.
Walk up Via Alloro away from the sea and go right into Vicolo della Neve all'Alloro. At the end of the Vicolo, go left and then bear right into Via Merlo.

6 Palazzo Mirto

This is a rare treat of a palazzo, in that it has preserved its original furnishings. The portal contains the coat of arms of the Filangeri family, who lived here until 1980 before it was donated to the state. The elegantly furnished drawing rooms and the theatrical courtyard garden are highlights.

Banyan trees in Piazza Marina

PALERMO'S 19TH-CENTURY HIGHLIGHTS

Piazza Verdi, with the renovated magnificence of Teatro Massimo, marks the start of the more elegant, modern part of the city. You visibly notice the greater space in the boulevards and squares of this area, where there is less traffic and bustle and a more sedate pace to life. Nothing exemplifies this more than the wide-open spaces of piazzas Castelnuovo and Ruggero Settimo, which are popular on Sundays with strolling families.

Known as La Città del Ottocento (City of the 1800s), this area contains examples from the last golden age of Sicilian architecture, as well as elegant outdoor cafés, designer boutiques and, in contrast, some pretty ugly modern apartment blocks and offices.

Viale della Libertà is especially striking, with numerous Art Deco buildings along its wide, tree-lined avenue. On Sundays, the main avenue is closed to traffic and is a popular place for strolling and bike-riding, very much becoming an 'outdoor living room' for the city's inhabitants.

Teatro Massimo

This magnificent building was restored back to its former glory in time for its centenary in 1997, and is symbolic of Palermo's regeneration over the last decade. It is the city's key venue for the arts, particularly opera, and boasts the largest indoor stage in Europe after the Paris Opera House. It was designed by Giovanni Battista Basile in the neoclassical style and finished in 1897. The climax of the film *The Godfather Part III*, starring Al Pacino, was staged on the steps here. Note the two beautifully restored Art Deco kiosks in front of the theatre.

Piazza Verdi. Tel: (091) 605 3580. www.teatromassimo.it.
Open: Tue–Sun 10am–3pm except during rehearsals. Admission charge includes a short guided tour (some tours in English).

Teatro Politeama Garibaldi

This impressive-looking theatre dominates Piazza Ruggero Settimo, and dates from the period of economic crisis in the later half of the 19th century. It was designed in the classical style by Giuseppe Damiani Almeyda, a young civil engineer, who finished it in 1874. The eye-catching façade consists of a triumphal arch topped by a bronze figure and chariots. It was intended as a daytime theatre for more populist entertainment such as acrobatics, an equestrian circus, comic plays and festivities, hence the name, derived from *polytheama* (a theatre for shows of many kinds). Cultural performances take place here.

Piazza Ruggero Settimo. Tel: (091) 605 3315. Open: during performances only. Tourist office will have full details of events and performances.

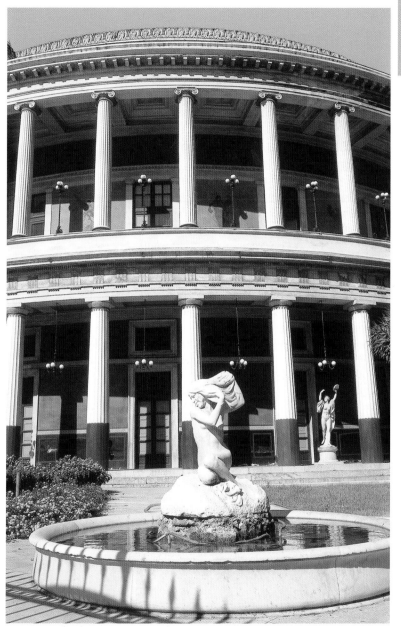

Side view of Teatro Politeama Garibaldi on Piazza Ruggero Settimo

Di Lampedusa and *The Leopard*

Giuseppe Tomasi di Lampedusa's novel *Il Gattopardo* (The Leopard) and the subsequent film directed by Luchino Visconti are recommended for anyone interested in modern Sicilian history and culture. The classic novel tells the story of an aristocratic family in the 1860s and their decline. The author was himself a Sicilian aristocrat who spent his youth at his family's properties in Palermo and the rugged interior of the island.

A film to live by

Visconti's 1963 film was described by director Martin Scorsese as 'one of the films I live by'. The film is a historical costume drama on a grand scale, and is seen as a requiem not only for the old Sicily, but also for a European film-making tradition based on ambition and grandeur.

The film describes the consequences of the reunification movement in Sicily at the time of Garibaldi's landing in Sicily. A world-weary nobleman, Prince Fabrizio (Burt Lancaster), knows that things will never be the same again. The film closes with a grand ball at the Donnafugata Palace, an isolated country estate. The famous ballroom sequence is said to symbolise the death throes of the aristocracy. Casa Ponteleone and Palazzo Gangi in the town of Ciminna in central Sicily were used as locations for the film. The actual Donnafugata is located in Santa Margherita Belice, in the Belice Valley south of Palermo (*see p71*).

Garibaldi, whose exploits feature in *The Leopard*, immortalised in stone in Trapani

A reclusive life

Giuseppe Tomasi di Lampedusa was born in Palermo in 1896, the son of the Duke of Parma. His ancestors had moved to Palermo in 1672, and quickly became an important family in the city.

Di Lampedusa was to grow up a very reclusive man, spending many hours alone in his ancestors' palaces in Via Lampedusa and their country estates. He took a diploma in Classical Studies, travelled a great deal, then returned to Palermo after being dismissed from military service.

Every day for the final ten years of his life, di Lampedusa took the same walk through Palermo. Many of the places he frequented can still be seen today and his route can easily be followed. The di Lampedusa family house is very near the Marionette Museum in Via Butera, which runs parallel to the sea just east of Piazza Marina, in La Kalsa district. Walking along Corso Vittorio Emanuele, he used to pass Piazza Marina, and then walk up the busy Via Roma. It was behind the intersection of Via Cavour and Via Roma where di Lampedusa lived as a boy. Just next to the Oratorio del Rosario di Santa Cita is di Lampedusa's birthplace, a grand palace that was bombed by the Allies during World War II, forcing the family to move to La Kalsa.

Di Lampedusa would take breakfast at cafés such as Café Caflish around Piazza Verdi, near the Teatro Massimo. He would frequent Flaccovio's bookshop every morning and buy books, his real passion in life. The owner of the shop tried to use his contacts to have *The Leopard* published, but failed. Across the road in Via Generale Magliocco, two blocks northwest of Teatro Massimo, is the old-fashioned-looking Pasticceria Mazzara, where di Lampedusa used to sit writing. It was here that he began to work on *The Leopard* towards the end of 1954, in an attempt to describe the life of his great-grandfather in the 1800s.

Di Lampedusa died in 1957 and was buried in the Cappuccini Cemetery in Palermo, where his wife joined him 25 years later. The novel was published as *Il Gattopardo* a year after his death, and was an immediate if unexpected success. It won its first literary prize in 1959 and was translated into English in 1960.

Parco Litterario Giuseppe Tomasi di Lampedusa, which also has a café, offers a free film about the life and work of the author, and on request organises tours of the city following in di Lampedusa's footsteps (*Vicolo della Neve all'Alloro 2. Tel: (091) 616 0796*).

PALERMO ENVIRONS

Visitors based in Palermo have a range of options to visit towns and other attractions in the area, and there are excellent transport links to places outside the capital. Included are sights that can be reached in one hour – by bus, car or train.

The closest attractions are the Capuchin Catacombs, just outside the city, and Monreale, a historic medieval town with a cathedral famous for its stunning Byzantine mosaics. Monreale Cathedral should be on everyone's itinerary, even if you are only in Palermo for a day or two. Nearer to the city centre are the green spaces and splendid views at Monte Pellegrino, and the beach at Mondello.

Castello della Zisa

This is worth visiting in conjunction with the catacombs outside the city, as they are very near to each other. The area is not particularly salubrious, but at least this 12th-century Norman castle has at last been restored after being left to decay for centuries. This was the main building in a royal park. The name comes from the Arabic *el aziz*, meaning 'splendid'. It is easy to imagine the luxuriousness of the ornate Sala della Fontana (Fountain Hall), the main reception room of the palace. William II enjoyed La Zisa as a summer residence, and he would have made the most of the oasis of gardens and fountains. It now houses an interesting museum of Saracen artisanship,

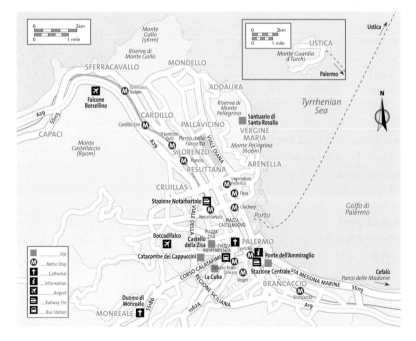

including a lovely bronze basin dating from the 13th century and Turkish-style screens.

Piazza Zisa, 1km (²/₃ mile) west of the city centre. Tel: (091) 652 0269. Open: Tue–Sun 9am–6.30pm. Take bus 124 from Piazza Ruggero Settimo in the city centre. Admission charge.

Catacombe dei Cappuccini (Capuchin Catacombs)

Despite the fact that this is quite a creepy, disturbing place, it is one of the most popular tourist spots in and around Palermo. These underground catacombs were used between the 17th and 19th centuries by the Capuchin monks to bury the rich and wealthy Palermitans who wanted to be embalmed. There are at least 8,000 people here, either mummified or as skeletons. The bodies are categorised by gender and profession, lined up in the badly lit, damp rooms, which only serve to heighten the macabre and scary atmosphere. One of the most chilling of the figures is a two-year-old girl who was embalmed so well that she seems almost alive still. Just follow the signs for the *bambina* (little girl).

Piazza Cappuccini 1, 1km (²/₃ mile) west of Palermo. Take bus 327 from Piazza Indipendenza. Tel: (091) 212 117. Open: Mon–Sat 9am–12.45pm & 3–5.45pm, Sun 9am–12.45pm. Admission charge.

La Cuba

This large square building, which looks like a defensive fortress, would have stood in the same ground as La Zisa. It is also Norman, but in the Fatimid style, dating from the late 12th century. In its heyday, it would have been surrounded by an artificial pond and used as a pavilion in which William II could while away hot afternoons. Little remains of its former glory now: it was converted into a cavalry barracks in the Bourbon era.

Corso Calatafimi 100, 1km (²/₃ mile) southwest of Porta Nuova. Tel: (091) 590 299. Tue–Sat 9am–6.30pm, Sun & holidays 9am–1pm. Admission charge.

Mondello

Outside Palermo and just a few kilometres north of Monte Pellegrino is the Palermitans' favourite beach; they

Detail of a column in Monreale Cathedral

The harbour at Mondello, with its colourful fishing boats

crowd the most popular section at Viale Regina Elena. Running alongside are lots of beachside restaurants and cafés that specialise in fresh seafood, while there is also plenty of opportunity to 'people-watch' along the boardwalk, where locals enjoy taking a stroll (*passeggiata*). Luckily, the beach stretches for 2km (1¼ miles), although in the summer it can barely accommodate all the local people who flock here.

11km (7 miles) north of Palermo. Take bus 806, or 833 in summer, from the Politeama Theatre or Viale della Libertà. Journey time: 30 mins.

The Palazzina Cinese in the Parco della Favorita

Monreale

Monreale is a charming town in the suburbs of Palermo, positioned on a mountain with great views over the valley. In fact, its name means 'royal mountain'.

Duomo

Begun in 1174, the cathedral's Norman façade is marked by massive lateral towers. The interior is regarded as one of the most beautiful in Sicily, and it does not disappoint. It is a blend of Arabic, Byzantine, Classical and Norman architectural influences that has stood the test of time remarkably well.

It is ironic that the motivation for creating this beautiful building was political. William II wanted to undermine the power of the archbishop of Palermo, Walter of the Mill, who was closely allied with the Pope in Rome.

William created an archbishopric in Monreale in 1183 and had the huge cathedral built, in a bold attempt to emphasise that he should be regarded as the ultimate authority.

The interior of the cathedral, often crowded with tour groups, is lit by cash-operated light boxes, so make sure you have change handy in case no one else obliges. The Byzantine mosaics cover most of the interior, a staggering total of more than 6,000sq m (64,600sq ft). Artists from Venice and the local areas took ten years to complete the mosaics, depicting stories from the Bible, saints and the Virgin and Child. The whole is dominated by the figure of Christ *Pantokrator* (All-Powerful) in the central apse.

Walk around the back to see the exterior of the apse, articulated with intricate stonework in lava and limestone.

Visitors can climb the tower, which has dizzying views over the town and valley. The beautiful cloister, which was part of the adjacent Benedictine monastery, is a mixture of Norman, Arab and Romanesque influences with around 200 exquisitely carved columns. *8km (5 miles) from Palermo. Take bus 389 or 309 from Piazza Indipendenza (20 mins). Open: daily 8.30am–1.30pm & 2.30–5.30pm (often closes for afternoon weddings). Admission charge for tower, cloisters and treasury only.*

Monte Pellegrino

This picturesque mountain, at 606m (1,988ft), has several attractions worth visiting. Even the drive here is very pleasant, and a good outing from the bustle of the city. The main place to visit is **Santuario di Santa Rosalia** (Sanctuary of St Rosalia), dedicated to the patron saint of Palermo. The daughter of a duke, she decided to live as a hermit in a cave, where her remains were found 500 years later in 1625. A chapel has been built over the entrance to the cave, and legend has it that the water trickling among the walls has miraculous properties.

From the cave, you can walk the 30 minutes to the top of the mountain, which has great views over the city. At the bottom of the mountain is Parco della Favorita (*see below*).

On the northern side of the mountain the Grotta dell'Addaura has cave drawings dating back to the Palaeolithic and Neolithic periods. It is worth checking at the tourist office beforehand to find out when the site is open to visitors.

Take bus 812 from the Politeama Theatre in Piazza Sturzo. The bus drops you at the Santuario di Santa Rosalia. Tel: (091) 540 326. Open: daily 7.30am–8pm. Free admission.

Parco della Favorita

Palermo's biggest park, which is 3km (nearly 2 miles) across, has several points of interest, both historic and contemporary. It is home to the city's football team, which plays at the stadium that also houses tennis courts and a modern sports centre. The edge of the park is dotted with impressive villas, used by the island's nobility as summer residences. Villa Niscemi is mentioned in Giuseppe Tomasi di Lampedusa's novel *The Leopard* (1958).

The most extravagant of these buildings is Palazzina Cinese, the summer residence of Ferdinand I during his period in exile. This flamboyant building, combining Chinese, Gothic, Egyptian and Arab architectural styles, was constructed in 1799. The equally impressive interior is due to reopen soon following a long period of restoration.

The park itself was originally a hunting reserve until Ferdinand I turned it into gardens. The park is split into two by intersecting roads, Viale Diana and Viale d'Ercole, at the crossroads of which is a marble fountain with a statue of Hercules. *Viale Diana, on the road to Mondello, 8km (5 miles) north of the city centre, Pallavicino district.*

Ponte dell'Ammiraglio

This well-preserved 12th-century limestone bridge looks rather incongruous without a river flowing under it. It once spanned the Oreto River before that was diverted. It is named after Roger II's *ammiraglio* (high admiral), George of Antioch, who built it in 1113. At a length of 75m (246ft), it has stood the test of time remarkably well.

Via dei Mille, just south of the city centre.

Ustica

Just 60km (37½ miles) off the coast of Palermo, this isolated volcanic island is a popular getaway for city residents and watersports fans, who are attracted by its good beaches and superb scuba-diving and snorkelling sites. The island has only 1,000 residents or so, but fits in many times more people during the summer months, especially in July and August, when the crowds can be unbearable.

Ustica's name derives from the Italian word for 'burned', because of the volcanic eruptions that have taken place here. The landscape of the island is striking due to its black volcanic rock. At only 9sq km (3½ sq miles), it is the emerged section of a huge volcano, which is mostly under water.

Historically, it has enjoyed mixed fortunes. In medieval times, it suffered at the hands of pirates and was used to house exiled prisoners in the 19th century. In 1980, a passenger jet crashed here; the cause is still a mystery, although some people suspect military involvement.

The town itself, which has the same name as the island, is basically just a port with a few restaurants, bars and tourist facilities. The promontory of Capo Falconara dominates the town. Here there are ruins of an old fort and excellent views over to the Sicilian mainland.

There is a Marine Reserve off the coast, designed to protect its superb seabeds, with some areas totally out of bounds. The Marine Reserve does organise some boat tours however. Highlights of boat tours around the island include visiting underwater caves such as Grotta Azzurra and Grotta delle Colonne. The most popular dive sites are around Secca Colombara and Punta Gavazzi.

60km (37½ miles) northwest of Palermo. Ferries and hydrofoils operate roughly once or twice daily from the Stazione Marittima in Palermo.

Ponte dell'Ammiraglio, Palermo

Northwest Sicily

In addition to the capital of the region, Palermo, the northwest of Sicily has much to offer the tourist: the most evocative Greek ruins on the island, some of the most beautiful stretches of coastline and a rugged interior populated with villages that exemplify the Sicilian way of life. And it's all within easy reach now that the airport south of Trapani at Birgi is open to commercial flights.

Northwest Sicily has been particularly influenced by different civilisations over the centuries, being situated near North Africa and Spain. The Elymians, Aeneas and his friends who fled burning Troy, founded Erice, Segesta and Entella. The Phoenicians settled in Mozia and founded a harbour town at Palermo. The Greeks and Romans followed, and the Arabs begun their conquest of the island at Marsala.

The ancient ruins at Segesta and Selinunte are not to be missed with their splendid temples in majestic

Local fishermen

settings. Trapani is an excellent base from which to explore the area and is an attractive town in its own right. Few visitors to the area would want to ignore the delightful medieval town of Erice, perched atop a hill with stunning views of the plains and sea. The coastline between Castellammare del Golfo and Mount Cofano is said to be the most beautiful on the island, with its heart being the Riserva Naturale dello Zingaro, the island's first nature reserve. The Egadi Islands (*Isole Egadi*), with excellent swimming and snorkelling, are just a short hop from Trapani's port, and popular with tourists and locals alike.

TRAPANI

Trapani is a major departure point for Pantelleria and Sardinia. While the city itself has few sights of note, it is an ideal base for visiting tourist attractions in the area such as Erice, the Egadi Islands, San Vito lo Capo, Segesta, Mozia and Marsala.

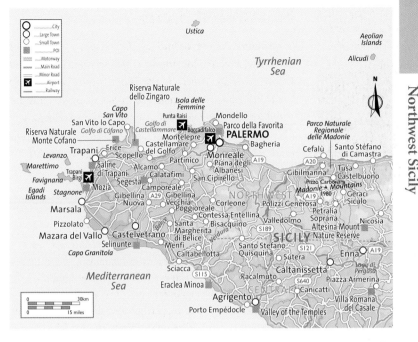

The city sits below the headland of Mount San Giuliano and has lovely views over the sea towards the Egadi Islands. It is positioned on a curved, slim promontory, which gave it its Greek name Drepanon (*drepane* means 'sickle'). Trapani flourished under the Carthaginians, who used it as a key port for trade and defence. It was captured by the Romans in 241 BC, and thereafter by a range of different conquerors, all of whom landed here on their way to capturing the rest of Sicily.

After nearly 400 years of obscurity, the city grew rich again, its wealth derived from tuna fishing and its shipyards. Like many other Sicilian harbour cities, it suffered Allied bombardments during World War II, damage that was not much improved by the building of ugly office and apartment tower blocks.

The town is bordered to the north and south by the sea. The main thoroughfare, Via Fardella, connects the modern city in the east with the charming historic centre. The most attractive part of the city is the medieval heart of the town, the *centro storico* (historic centre), which has a North African feel to it. The busiest street at the weekends is Via Garibaldi, also known as Rua Nova (New Road), which is at the northern end of the town centre.

Dating from the Aragonese period in the 18th century, Trapani is lined with churches, old palaces, shops and cafés, and it is along here that most of the action takes place on weekend nights.

The pedestrianised main street is Corso Vittorio Emanuele, which sparks into life in the early evening, when shops reopen and inhabitants spill on to this pleasant Baroque street for a stroll. The main churches can be found along here. There is good shopping along the Corosin Via Torrearsa and in and around the Piazzetta della Cuba.
Tourist office: Via San Francesco d'Assisi 27. Tel: (0923) 54 1183. Open: Mon & Tue, Thur–Sat 8am–1pm, Wed 8am–1pm & 3–6pm.

Cattedrale di San Lorenzo
The cathedral has an attractive Baroque façade by Giovanni Biagio Amico, and was built on the site of a 14th-century church. The most notable item inside is a painting of the Crucifixion by Giacomo Lo Verde, a local artist.

Boats small and large at Trapani port

Corso Vittorio Emanuele. Tel: (0923) 23 362. Open: daily 8.30am–12pm & 4.30–8pm.

Chiesa del Purgatorio
This church houses perhaps the most important relics in the town. The Misteri are 20 life-size wooden figures depicting Christ's Passion in graphic detail. They date from the 18th century. The church itself is from the 17th century but the inside is medieval. The atmosphere is enhanced by the incense. *Just by the Stazione Marittima, one block up from Piazza Garibaldi. Open: daily 10am–12pm & 5–7pm.*

Museo Nazionale Pepoli
Next to the Santuario dell'Annunziata, a bus journey east of the historic centre, is this important regional museum. Housed in a former monastery, the art on display is based around the private collection of Count

Agostino Pepoli, who donated it to the city. Items shown include ceramics, coral jewellery, clocks, tapestries and paintings from the 12th to the 18th century. The collection also includes Titian's *San Francesco con Stigmata*. *Via Conte Agostino Pepoli 200. Tel: (0923) 55 3269. Open: Mon–Sat 9am–1.30pm, Sun 9am–12.30pm. Admission charge.*

Santuario dell'Annunziata

This is perhaps Trapani's most important sight, next to Museo Nazionale Pepoli. This 14th-century church contains a masterpiece of Gothic sculpture, *Madonna and Child* by Nino Pisano, as well as some superb reliefs by the Gagini brothers. Although the church was redesigned in the 18th century, it still retains its impressive rose window and Gothic portal. *Via Conte Agostino Pepoli. Tel: (0923) 53 9184. Open: daily 7am–noon & 4–8pm. Free admission. Take bus 24, 25 or 30 from Corso Vittorio Emanuele and get off at Villa Pepoli.*

Santuario dell'Annunziata, Trapani

ERICE

Medieval Erice is one of the most beautiful towns in Sicily. Its enchanting position at the top of the hill is pure picture-postcard. It is a magnet for tour groups, and day-trippers arriving in coaches or via the short funicular ride straight up the mountain face.

It is certainly worth spending half a day wandering the cobblestoned medieval streets of Erice. In the evening, the town is enchanting, and in winter, often enveloped in an eerie mist. There are vertigo-inducing vistas from the cliffs at several vantage points, which give panoramic views across the plains and towards the northwest promontory of Sicily, San Vito lo Capo.

A settlement was first built here 3,000 years ago. It became the ancient city of Eryx, named after the mythical ruler of the Elymian people, an Anatolian mountain race who also founded Segesta. The Phoenicians, Greeks and Romans valued the spot, as it was an important religious site associated with fertility goddesses, while the Arabs saw it as an important strategic foothold. After the Normans captured the city, it was known as Monte San Giuliano – until 1934, when Mussolini decreed a return to its Latin name.

If you have not already tried fish couscous, a speciality of this region, do so here. Don't miss the *dolci Ericini*, the elaborate local sweets renowned throughout the island. If you enjoy looking at churches, indulge yourself: there are apparently 60 churches in this little town alone.

Castello Pepoli e Venere

Dominating the southeast corner of the town is this Norman castle, which was built on an isolated rock in the 12th century, on the site of the temple dedicated to Venus Erycina. You can enter via the tower, the only remaining

The Castello Pepoli e Venere at Erice

original part of the castle, which was used as a prison and watchtower. The fortifications within are known as the Torri del Balio, and they were once the headquarters of the Norman governor. He is also remembered by the pretty 19th-century gardens, Giardini del Balio, which bear his name. The spectacular views from here extend out to the Egadi Islands on a clear day.
At the southeastern tip of the town, at the end of Viale Conte Pepoli, a few metres up the hill from the funicular station. Open: daily 8am–7pm. Free admission.

The bells of Chiesa Madre, Erice

Chiesa Madre

This Gothic church has a stunning rose window over the main entrance, facing the separate campanile (bell tower). Built in 1314 using stone from the Temple of Venus, it was restored in 1865: the interior has good chapels and an interesting ceiling. The campanile was originally a lookout tower, and offers great views over the medieval town on one side and the Gulf of Trapani on the other.
*Via Vito Carvini.
Tel: (0923) 86 9123. Open: daily 10am–7pm. Admission charge.*

Cyclopean Walls

Also known as the Punic Walls, these date from the Phoenician period (around 8th century BC), indicated by the Phoenician letters carved into them. The upper part of the walls were added by the Normans. You can follow the walls from Porta Spada to Porta Trapani on the northern side of town. It was at Porta Spada that the local French Angevin rulers were slaughtered during the 13th-century Sicilian Vespers.
Just north of Chiesa Madre.

Museo Civico Cordici

Located in the main square of the town, the museum upstairs displays archaeological finds from the necropolis and the surrounding area, including a small head of Venus from the 4th century BC. Another highlight is *Annunciation*, a sculpture by Antonello Gagini dating from the early 16th century. The museum was named after Antonio Cordici, a local historian from the 17th century.
Piazza Umberto I. Tel: (0923) 86 9172. Open: Mon & Thur 8.30am–1.30pm & 3–5pm, Tue, Wed & Fri 8.30am–1.30pm, Sat 9am–1pm. Free admission.

NORTHWEST COAST

Between Marsala and Trapani is a stretch of coastline first exploited for sea-salt extraction by the Phoenicians. This can be explored easily if you have your own transport. Offshore lie the popular Egadi Islands, easily accessed from the mainland.

You will see the famous *saline* (saltpans) from far away, even from the hilltop at Erice. Large mounds of salt are covered with terracotta tiles to dry in the sun. There are also some windmills still standing, which used to supply the energy to move water from basin to basin and to the mills that ground the salt. The **Stagnone di Marsala** and **Saline di Trapani** marshes have been made a nature reserve in order to protect the seawater from pollution and maintain its rich variety of water-bird species. Also situated in the Stagnone lagoon are the archaeological remains of **Mozia**, on the tiny island of San Pantaleo, which is a pleasant boat ride from the shore.

A windmill at Saline di Trapani

Egadi Islands

These islands are very popular in the summer, when they are inundated with Sicilian families on day trips, who come to swim and sunbathe on the beaches. The archipelago of the Isole Égadi is made up of three small islands: Favignana, Levanzo and Marettimo. Historians suggest that they were linked to the mainland more than half a million years ago but that, as the sea level rose, they became isolated from the rest of Sicily. It was off this coast that the Romans under Catullus defeated the Carthaginian fleet in 241 BC to take the islands.

Favignana is the largest and most developed of the islands, with a small town and good tourist facilities. It was the scene of the famous *mattanza*, the slaughter of tuna each May and June. Because of dwindling numbers of tuna due to overfishing, the annual harvest has been interrupted.

Levanzo has excellent beaches and fascinating prehistoric cave paintings that can be visited in the Grotta del Genovese. The port area looks strikingly like a Greek island village, with white-painted buildings and blue shutters. The island of Marettimo is the least developed, but is good for walking and swimming.
Regular hydrofoil service from Trapani.

Mozia and the Whitaker Museum

These Phoenician ruins are situated on the small island of San Panataleo, in the Stagnone lagoon. Joseph Whitaker

Cala Dogana Harbour, Levanzo, Egadi Islands

began excavating the ancient city of Mozia from 1913; he was an amateur archaeologist and English wine merchant, whose family made their fortune from Marsala wine. He bought the island, building a villa there and a museum to house his finds. Very little remains of the city, as it was destroyed by Dionysius the Elder in 397 BC. You can visit the remains of the ancient fortified port and dry dock while enjoying the picturesque scenery.

The small but fascinating Whitaker Museum houses Phoenician and Greek objects and the splendid 5th-century-BC Greek marble *Giovietto di Mozia* (Young Man from Mozia), one of the most famous sculptures in Sicily.

San Pantaleo Island (boats from the dock at the Saline Ettore e Infersa). Tel: (0923) 712 598. Open: daily 9.15am–1.30pm & 2.30–6.30pm; closes at 3pm in winter. Admission charge.

Saline Ettore e Infersa

Located in a working windmill, the small museum houses traditional equipment, the old grist mill and a small shop selling salts harvested on site. There is an informative didactic film (upon special request and for a fee).

On the Stagnone, midway between Trapani and Marsala. Tel: (0923) 733 003. Open: Apr–Oct daily 9.30am–7.30pm.

MARSALA

Sun-baked Marsala grew from a Phoenician settlement and presents a low profile with Baroque buildings and wide piazzas built from a local golden stone. English merchants companies set up outposts here during the late 1700s as shipping fortified Marsala wine to northern Europe became a successful business venture. A reminder of the their presence is the mother church dedicated to San Tommaso di Canterbury. The mercenary Giuseppe Garibaldi put the town on the modern map by choosing it as his entry point into Sicily and starting point for his red-shirted Army of a Thousand, which eventually led to the unification of Italy. *Tourist information office: Via XI Maggio 100. Tel: (0923) 71 4097. Open: Mon–Sat 8am–2pm & 3–8pm, Sun 9am–noon.*

Baglio Anselmi Archaeological Museum

The prize object of this collection is an enormous Punic warship, which was sunk offshore and discovered in 1971. There is interesting material concerning the ship, its raising from the sea floor and the objects found on board. From here, you can access the excavations of the Roman settlement, though it is currently closed for restoration. *Lungomare Boe. Tel: (0923) 952 535. Open: daily 9am–6pm. Admission charge.*

Garibaldi Museum

The permanent exhibition celebrates the Risorgimento and Garibaldi's entry

MARSALA WINE

Modern Marsala was developed in the 18th century by English merchants who fortified the local wine for conservation during shipment to England. During the 20th century, commercial bottlings gave it a reputation as a cooking wine, but since the 1970s producers dedicated to tradition, *terroir* and quality have been making Marsala of excellent quality. Following tradition, this nectar of indigenous white grapes matures *a solera* (new vintages are used to top off large casks of older vintages, resulting in a blend of vintages of very old founding date). Look for bottles with the historic Florio label or from Marco de Bartoli who makes Marsala as well as sublime, traditional, non-fortified wine.

into Marsala. There are uniforms, weapons, photographs, documents and even an armchair in which Garibaldi is said to have rested after entering the city. *Via L Anselmi Correale. Tel: (0923) 718 741. Open: Tue–Sun 9am–1pm & 4–8pm.*

Mazara del Vallo

Historically an Arab centre, it has become one again with an influx of Tunisian fishermen. Within the Kasbah, the **Museo del Satiro** houses a fabulous 4th-century-BC Greek bronze *Dancing Satyr* hauled up from an ancient shipwreck by a fishing boat in 1998 (*Chiesa di Sant'Egidio, Piazza Plebiscito. Tel: (0923) 933 917. Open: daily 9am–6pm. Admission charge*). *8 miles (13km) southeast of Marsala.*

THE BELICE VALLEY

The Belice river valley runs roughly from Palermo to Selinunte, passing through the island's rugged interior and villages that give a good idea of real life in Sicily. A massive earthquake in 1968 levelled five villages and heavily damaged many more. Driving through the zone you will pass craggy mountains, cultivated valleys and ghost-town ruins left by the quake.

Poggioreale

The remains of the charming old town of Poggioreale can be seen in the countryside above the new village along the SP 5 road. Modern Poggioreale was built in the 1980s and has a small ethnographic museum full of implements used in everyday life not that long ago (*Corso Umberto I, Piazza Pertini. Open: Mon–Fri 8am–1.30pm*). The small shop and cheese-making facility of the Azienda Agricola Laura Giocondo is also worth visiting (*Corso Umberto I, 30. Tel: (320) 483 5107. Open: daily 8am–6pm, call in advance for guided visit*).

Eleven kilometres (7 miles) further along the SP 5 road from the old town of Poggioreale stood the village of Gibellina. Its unstable remains have been razed, but the ancient village is commemorated with the Creto di Burri, a moving installation of enormous concrete slabs that follow the shape of the old urban plan. *Poggioreale is 500m (¹/₃ mile) west of the SS 624.*

Santa Margherita Belice

The big villa in the town centre was the country estate of Giuseppe Tomasi di Lampedusa's grandmother. The author spent his summers here and this was the house on which the literary and film version of the palace at Donnafugata was based (*see pp54–5*). *On the SS 188, 5km (3 miles) from the SS 624, south of Poggioreale.*

Poggioreale lies on the slope of the Belice Valley

SEGESTA

Many people who visit this ancient abandoned city come on day trips from Palermo – it is just an hour's drive away – or stop here on their way to Trapani and Erice. Not all of this once-powerful city has been excavated, but it is still worth the trip. The temple itself is in a wonderful position, as is the theatre, isolated in the countryside with wondrous views of the hills and coast. There is little shade at the site though, and it gets very hot (even in winter).

Segesta was involved in political alliances of one kind or another through much of its history, in increasingly desperate attempts not to be destroyed by the powers of each era, namely Carthage, Rome and Greece. Originally settled by the Elymians, it was part of the Greek Empire, signing a treaty with Athens in 426 BC while other Sicilian cities fought. Segesta constantly

The Roman theatre at Segesta

vied with Selinunte for supremacy, and sought help from Carthage to defeat its enemy in 409 BC. Segesta also benefited from Carthaginian support against another rival city, Siracusa, and against the Romans. However, Segesta's rulers had a sudden change of heart and made a secret alliance with Rome. The Carthaginian troops stationed in its city were murdered in a breathtaking act of treachery and ingratitude.

By the time the Saracens took the city, it was already in decline, and was eventually abandoned around the 13th century. Segesta's Doric temple and theatre have miraculously survived centuries of earthquakes and wars. This is one of the best-preserved Greek sites in the world.

Temple

This amazing Doric temple dates from 430 BC, but it was never completed. There are many theories to explain this, one of which is that the non-Greek population built it to gain the military support of Athens. Once Athens lost to Siracusa, Segesta turned to Carthage for protection and abandoned work on the temple. The huge temple, 60m (197ft) high with 36 columns, was left with unfluted columns, no roof and no *cella* (the interior space that would have housed the cult statue).

Theatre

This beautifully situated theatre dates from the 3rd century BC, being carved out of the rock on the slopes of Monte

Barbaro, 400m (1,312ft) above sea level. There are 20 tiers of seating arranged in a semicircle, capable of holding more than 3,000 spectators. It is difficult to imagine a more dramatic backdrop to the theatre, with hills and the sea at Castellamare del Golfo spreading out into the distance. The acoustics are perfect: a person speaking on the stage can be heard clearly from the higher seats. Performances of Greek tragedies and concerts are held here each summer.

Tel: (0923) 808 111. Open: daily 9am–7pm (last admission 6pm). 32km (20 miles) from Trapani. Buses and trains from Trapani take 30 mins. There are also buses and trains from Palermo. Admission charge; extra charge for shuttle to theatre.

Northwest Sicily

The huge Doric temple at Segesta was never completed

SELINUNTE

Because of its vulnerable position as the westernmost Greek colony on the island, it was in Selinunte's best interest to construct an imposing image. Whether approached by land or sea, enormous, gleaming temples were visible from afar, attesting to the city's power and wealth. Despite sieges, earthquakes and centuries of abandon, its spectacular site and the good fortune of never having been built upon by successive civilisations have resulted in the ruins of Selinunte being extremely impressive.

History

Selinunte was founded as a colony of Megara Hyblea in 628 BC. It is sited ideally on an easily defended plateau bordered by two rivers, the estuaries of which formed natural ports (but have since silted up). The plateau provided safe residential quarters to the north and a fortress-like location to the south where the Acropolis was raised above a sheer drop to the sea. Inland, the earth was fertile and flat allowing for the cultivation of grains and olives. Selinunte was a thriving city with a population of 100,000 and a strong economy based on agriculture and trade. Its coins bear an image of the wild celery plant (*selinon*), after which the city was named. Temples were constructed inside the fortified Acropolis and in two sacred areas to the east and west of the city.

Selinunte waged frequent war to maintain its autonomy and expand its domain in hostile territory. It formed an alliance with Carthage during the 5th century BC but remained neutral in the Greek–Carthaginian War, which ended in Carthaginian defeat at the Battle of Himera. Perennial border struggles with Segesta led to Selinunte's downfall and set off a power struggle that changed the political face of the entire Mediterranean. After Himera, with Carthage held at bay, Selinunte allied itself with powerful Siracusa. Segesta in turn asked Athens for support and Athens accepted, taking the opportunity to go on the offensive against Siracusa. In 415 BC, Athens launched the Great Sicilian Expedition only to suffer a surprising defeat. Although Siracusa was victorious, it was greatly weakened, thus opening the door for Carthaginian re-entry to the island. Segesta quickly changed allegiance, seeking protection from Carthage who, under Hannibal, pounded Selinunte to the ground. After a nine-day seige in 409 BC, Selinunte was sacked, burned and almost its entire population massacred.

The few remaining survivors found themselves in Carthaginian territory when in 368 BC Siracusa signed a treaty with Carthage marking the border well to the east of Selinunte. A small Punic settlement lived within the Acropolis walls, building on top of the Greek remains until they were transferred to Lilybaeum (Marsala) during the First

Punic War in 250 BC. There is further evidence of small Roman and Byzantine communities, but Selinunte was quickly forgotten, buried under sand dunes and maquis.

Eastern Hill

The Eastern sacred zone was home to three Doric temples and their sacrificial altars, built during the 6th and 5th centuries BC.

Unlike other Sicilian Doric temples, the temples of Selinunte were decorated with sculpture and colour. The remarkably carved *metopes* from the entablature of Temple E are in Palermo's archaeological museum. All Selinunte's temples were covered with whitewash and their entablatures painted yellow, red and blue; fragments of colour still survive.

Temple E, re-erected in the 1950s, was built in 460–450 BC and perhaps dedicated to Hera, sister and wife of Zeus. It was built in the Doric style with a single row of columns all the way around, 6 columns across the front and 15 down the sides, and an interior *cella* where the cult statue was housed.

Temple F, smaller in scale with 6 x 14 columns, was perhaps dedicated to Dionysius or possibly Athena, in which case the three temples of the Eastern Hill would have been dedicated to the triad of Greek gods: Hera, Athena and Zeus.

(*Cont. on p78*)

The famous Temple E in Selinunte, dedicated perhaps to Hera, goddess of marriage

Walk: Ancient Selinunte

Selinunte is the largest archaeological park in Europe. There is a lot of distance to cover and the sun can be merciless, so come prepared and consider taking advantage of the shuttle service.

Allow about three hours, depending on how much time you spend walking about and if you walk or take the shuttle between sites.

Coming out of the ticket area (bottled water available) to the left, for an extra fee hire a navetta *(shuttle) that will stop first at the Eastern Hill, or walk to the right towards the Eastern Hill.*

1 Eastern Hill, Temples E, F and G

First approach the reconstructed Temple E, a supreme example of the harmonious simplicity of the Doric style. Many of the fluted columns retain traces of their original whitewash.

Pass the remains of Temple F to the third set of ruins, the massive Temple G. Some columns are complete while others have not been fluted. Notice square holes in the column drums where wooden dowels were inserted in order to help fix one drum on top of another. Look out for U-shaped channels that were carved into the sides of the stones to allow for ropes to pass through, facilitating their movement and positioning.

Walk or take the shuttle to the Acropolis.

2 Acropolis

Just in front of the small museum (containing artefacts from the site) is a stone slab with three openings. This was used in a shop for measuring quantities of dry goods.

Walk up the road following the right side of the stylobates (continuous base supporting a row of columns) of the ruins of Temples O and A.

3 Temple A

This was one of the last temples built in Selinunte in *c.* 480 BC. It is known for two spiral staircases that led from the cella into the *attic* (the storey above the cornice), the remains of which are still visible, and for the mosaic floors that were added during Punic times.

Proceed between remains of sacred altars and stoa (coverd walkway) towards the re-erected columns of Temple C.

4 Temple C and the 12 Shops

Here on the highest point of the Acropolis, Temple C was dedicated to

Apollo. The columns of the north side were re-erected in the 1920s. Directly in front of you is a row of 12, two-storey shops with staircases extant.

Go left, passing between the stylobates of Temples C (with columns standing) and D. When you get to the end of Temple D, go right on the main north–south road to reach the North Gate.

5 North Gate

Standing inside the gate notice that the massive fortifications were hastily reinforced after the seige by Hannibal in 409 BC. The exterior layer is distinct from the more orderly interior wall and contains stones taken from buildings on the Acropolis. Red stains are from ancient fire damage. From here, look out over the ruins of a moat, military installations and towards the residential area.

Turn round and walk down the main road towards the sea to return to the Acropolis entrance. Your visit can end here; otherwise, walk or take the shuttle to the Sanctuary of Malophoros (30 minutes' walk or a shuttle ride).

6 Sanctuary of Malophoros

The remains here are of sacred areas mostly dedicated to the chthonic fertility goddesses. More than 5,000 small terracotta votive statuettes of female figures were found here. Water for sacred rites was channelled from a spring through the middle of the site.

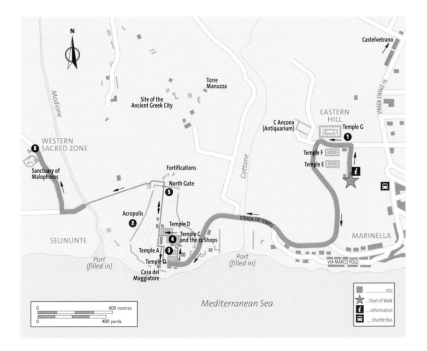

The rocky coastline of the Golfo di Castellammare

Colossal Temple G was built like the Parthenon with 8 x 17 columns and a wide, open-air *cella*. Because it was used as the city's treasury and due to its sheer size, scholars lean towards a dedication to Zeus, king of the gods. This is the second-largest temple in Sicily (after the Olympieion at Agrigento) and one of the largest temples in the entire Greek world. Each column was around 16m (52ft) tall and measured 3.4m (11ft) at the base. Begun in 530 BC, the temple seems to have been unfinished (although open for worship) at the time of the city's destruction in 409 BC.

Acropolis

Naturally divided into two zones, the southern end formed the citadel, the fortified site of Selinunte's civic and religious buildings, meeting places and shops and it is this area that has been almost completely excavated. With the sea as backdrop, walk among the ruins

of six temples, their altars, stoa, shops and instruments used for everyday life, which are displayed in a sort of open-air antiquarium. The main north–south road leads to the heavily fortified North Gate, beyond which are the ruins of the extensive and mostly unexcavated residential section.

Western Sacred Zone, Sanctuary of Malophoros

This area is a half-hour walk from the Acropolis. Used for sacred rites since the founding of Selinunte in the 7th century BC, the sanctuaries of this zone are related to the chthonic deities, the goddesses of the Underworld. The earliest of these sacred structures were small enclosures without colonnades. Later temples were built for rites associated with Malophoros, another name for Demeter, and Zeus Meilichios. Temple M was connected to the Acropolis by a wide processional road and it is presumed that rites were carried out here by funeral cortèges on their way to the necropoli located further to the west.

Parco Archaeologico di Selinunte. Tel: (092) 446 251/446 277. Open: daily 9am–7pm (last admission 6pm). Admission charge; extra fee for shuttle service.

GOLFO DI CASTELLAMMARE

This section of coastline, especially the west side of the Gulf of Castellammare, is one of the most beautiful in Sicily. There are rocky beaches, coves and sparkling clear waters. This area can be reached easily via the A29 from Palermo, which hugs the coast and then drops down just a few kilometres west of Castellammare del Golfo, which is the first stop for many visitors to the region. This town has a 17th-century Aragonese castle, quaint medieval streets and a lively port with bars and restaurants.

Scopello

Next along the coast heading west is this lovely village located high above the coastline, a good base for exploring the area. A delicious local speciality is *pane consatu*, a sandwich filled with fresh ingredients (*see p157*), available from the only bakery in the village.

The Tonnara di Scopello

The Tonnara is a tuna-fishing complex that dates from the 13th century. It closed in the 1980s with the demise of Sicily's tuna industry. It is now a surprisingly pretty and tranquil site, with a small shingle beach and luscious blue waters. The cove here is surrounded by *faraglioni* (rock towers) jutting out of the sea.

Riserva Naturale dello Zingaro

This tranquil nature reserve consists of steep mountains sloping down towards 7km (4^1/$_2$ miles) of pristine coastline. With an area of 1,600ha (3,900 acres), it is a paradise for birds, with 40 different species, including Bonelli's eagle and golden eagles. The park was established in 1980, and is ideal for exploring on foot or horseback. There are five marked footpaths, the shortest being 6km (4 miles), which goes from Scopello to Tonarella dell'Uzzo. Worth seeking out is the Grotta dell'Uzzo, a cave where human skeletons dating

Tonnara di Scopello

THE CORLEONE MAFIA

Ironically, Corleone became the Mafia capital of Sicily only several years after Coppola's film of 1972. It was Corleonese Totò Riina, renowned for his brutality, who took control of the Sicilian Mafia in the 1980s and who was responsible for the killings of judges Falcone and Borsellino. He was arrested and sent to prison, as were his sons and his successor as boss of bosses, Bernardo Provenzano. An anti-Mafia faction in Corleone managed to force a change in Italian law so that land confiscated from the Mafia could be worked by local farming cooperatives. The courageous leaders of the cooperative Libera Terra have taken full advantage of this possibility and now market olive oil, pasta, wine and other products throughout Italy under the Libera Terra label.

back 12,000 years have been found. Paths lead down to romantic coves with pebble beaches.

The entrance to the reserve is 2km (1¼ miles) northwest of Scopello. Tel: (0924) 35 108. Open: daily 7am–7.30pm (winter 8am–4pm). Admission charge.

San Vito lo Capo

Beyond the reserve, at the northernmost tip on this section of coastline, is San Vito lo Capo, a promontory that plunges into the sea. At the end of Via Savoia is a stunning beach with white sand, which is highly popular in the summer. September is a particularly busy time, with a couscous festival held here every year. The only other noteworthy site in town is the 13th-century Chiesa di San Vito.

SOUTH AND EAST OF PALERMO
Corleone

Visitors thinking of including this town in their itinerary because of the link to the *Godfather* films should think again. The film-makers felt that Corleone was too developed to be used as a location, and there is little to see here in terms of a link to the films.

Corleone's shady past is well hidden from today's visitors. Overlooking a fertile valley, it is a pleasant town to stroll around. Its ancient cobbled streets have a scattering of bars and trattorias, as well as a hotel. This medieval town was founded by the Moors as Qur la yun in the 9th century, and has a well-preserved historical centre. The only real sights in the town are the well-maintained churches of Chiesa Madre and Chiesa di Santa Rosalia, the latter dating from the 17th century and housing an excellent painting of *St John the Evangelist* by Velázquez (1599–1660). There is also a museum dedicated to the Mafia, although it is more of an 'anti-Mafia' museum.

Parco Naturale Regionale delle Madonie

This picturesque nature reserve incorporates the Madonie mountain range and a large part of Palermo province. It is a highly popular region with Sicilians, both as a day trip from Palermo in the summer for picnicking and hiking in cool mountain temperatures, and also in the winter where it is the only place other than

Etna where skiing is possible. The highest peak is Pizzo Carbonara; at 1,980m (6,500ft), it is second in height only to Mount Etna.

Covering 40,000ha (98,844 acres) south of Cefalù, the park was given status as a nature reserve in 1989. It includes several towns, villages, farms and vineyards, and is a good region to explore at leisure.

Gibilmanna

Of all villages in the Madonie this is the nearest to Cefalù, making it popular with tourists who have limited time in the park. The main attraction is the lovely view from the belvedere in front of the 17th-century church, which extends over the mountains. There is an elaborately decorated shrine of the Virgin Mary nearby at the Santuario di Gibilmanna, which attracts pilgrims.
5km (3 miles) south of Cefalù.

Petralia Soprana

This is the highest village in the Madonie mountains, and sits perched above a tree line of pines. The quaint atmosphere may have something to do with the historic medieval houses that have been left unplastered. The name derives from the Italian word *sopra* ('on' or 'above') and the Arabic name *Batraliah*. A church that should not be missed is Chiesa di Santa Maria di Loreto, a beautiful 18th-century building at the end of Via Loreto, off the main square, Piazza del Popolo.
27km (17 miles) south of Cefalù. From

The countryside near Corleone

Palermo, drive southwards from the coast on the A19, continuing for 23km (14 miles) before turning left, signposted to Castellana Sicula.

Polizzi Generosa

This is a perfect place to start a trek from, or to just wander round. It has many churches dotted around and is a charming town, often shrouded in mist. Built around a fortress in Norman times, Frederick II gave the town the name *generosa* (generous) in the early 13th century. The main attraction is the Chiesa Madre, containing some fine religious paintings.
17km (11 miles) west of Petralia Soprana, very near the A19.

CEFALÙ

The classy medieval seaside town of Cefalù, with its busy beach, excellent shopping and impressive monuments is emerging as a rival to Taormina as a quaint but upmarket destination for well-heeled visitors. It is not a big town, so it is possible to see the main sights in a day, although it is worth staying overnight to enjoy the lovely beach, right at the foot of the historical centre. It is picturesque, sitting at the foot of a huge crag called La Rocca (the castle), and has an impressive cathedral. During the peak summer months, prices hit the roof and the town is flooded with tourists.

The earliest settlement here was said to have been established in the 5th century BC by the Greeks. It was known as Kephalos (from the Greek for horse, the crag above the town resembling a horse's head). The town layout is pretty much as it was in the 5th century BC. When the Arabs invaded in the 8th century, many residents fled to seek refuge at the top of La Rocca.

Roger II ordered the cathedral to be built 50 years or so after the Normans captured the city from the Arabs, but the town declined after Roger's death. *Regional tourist information office. Corso Ruggero 7. Tel: (0921) 421 050. Open: Mon–Sat 8am–8pm.*

Beach

This beach is one of the best situated on the island. It lies just below the town, and has a row of restaurants overlooking it; these become packed on summer nights. The boardwalk is a popular place for strolling residents and visitors alike. The beach itself has fine golden sand, with lots of room in the summer for the crowds of visitors who cram it. Deckchairs and umbrellas can be rented in the summer. At times, *lo scirocco* (the wind from North Africa) swirls across the beach, making sun-worshippers run for cover.

Corso Ruggero

Corso Ruggero, running north to south, is the town's main street; it is where the most expensive shops and restaurants are located. It is busy at all hours of the day and night, as it is the main route of choice for visitors exploring the town. It hasn't changed much since Roman times. Later on in the town's history, it divided the wealthy quarter, uphill to the east, from the lower classes further downhill. The road starts at

SYMBOLS OF A BITTER RIVALRY

Legend has it that Cefalù's Duomo (cathedral) was built as a result of Roger II's tempestuous relationship with the archbishop in Palermo, Walter of the Mill. Walter was a strong supporter of the Pope, whereas Roger wanted to restrict the power and prestige of the papacy on the island. In building this mighty cathedral outside Palermo, Roger hoped to upstage the archbishop, who had just built the Capella Palatina in the Palazzo dei Normanni in Palermo. It is not certain who had the last laugh, however, as Roger II – in contravention of his wish to be buried in Cefalù – was laid to rest in Palermo's cathedral.

Piazza Garibaldi, a central point in the town, from where you can walk up to La Rocca, walk down to the beach, or walk northwards to the main medieval quarter. It ends at Piazza Crispi, downhill by the sea defences of the 17th-century Capo Marchiafava.

Duomo

This impressive Norman cathedral dominates the square below, which is a great public area, a popular meeting point with a number of restaurants and cafés. The interior is worth visiting, if only to admire the magnificent Byzantine mosaics, which predate those at Monreale Cathedral by 20–30 years. The figure of *Christ Pantokrator* (All-powerful Christ) in the central apse is especially skilfully produced.

The cathedral was built in 1131 by Roger II and has a monastery and

Cefalù's historic waterfront, with La Rocca in the background

Beach heaven near Cefalù town

cloister next door. Historians do not believe that the cathedral was ever completed. The painted cross suspended in the central apse dates from the 15th century, while another highlight is a 16th-century statue by Antonello Gagini.
Piazza del Duomo. Tel: (0921) 922 021. Open: daily 8am–7pm. Free admission.

Museo Mandralisca

This spectacular small museum is best known for housing the masterpiece by Antonello da Messina, *Portrait of an Unknown Man*, 1465. This painting is worth the entrance fee in itself. The collection also includes delightful Greek ceramics, rare coins and Arab pottery, as well as a library and art gallery. The collection was established by Baron di Mandralisca in the 19th century.
Via Mandralisca 13. Tel: (0921) 42 1547. www.museomandralisca.it. Open: daily 9am–7pm. Admission charge.

Palazzo Osterio Magno

Just to the side of the tourist office is this impressive building, perhaps the most important historic building in town. It is said to be where Roger II stayed when visiting the city, hence the name, which means 'great guesthouse'. It is composed of two buildings of different dates: one is late 13th century and one is 14th century. Now heavily renovated, it has lost some of its charm and is sometimes overlooked by visitors. *On the corner of Corso Ruggero & Via Amendola. Open: only for temporary art exhibitions.*

La Rocca

This huge crag towers over the town, imposing and slightly sinister. At 268m (879ft) high, it has been one of the few unchangeable things in the town's history. Climbing up the rock is a popular walk with energetic visitors. In fact, it takes less than 30 minutes to climb to the Tempio di Diana (Temple of Diana) halfway up. This dates from the 4th century BC and was a religious site used by the cult of Hercules. The remains of some Norman fortifications lie below it, while little is left of the castle that once stood at the summit. The views are the best thing about the climb, looking over the town and coast.

Cefalù's Piazza del Duomo and 12th-century cathedral

Walk: Around Cefalù town centre

This walk starts at the Palazzo Osterio Magno, opposite the tourist office, which has good maps and information about the town. Be warned that the last section of the walk involves a steep climb.

Allow two to three hours.

1 Palazzo Osterio Magno

Although heavily renovated and only open for temporary art exhibitions, this is still an imposing building. Built in the 13th and 14th centuries, it was home to

the powerful Ventimiglia family.
Walk down Corso Ruggero for about 200m (220yds) until you reach the picturesque Piazza del Duomo. Turn right to the Duomo.

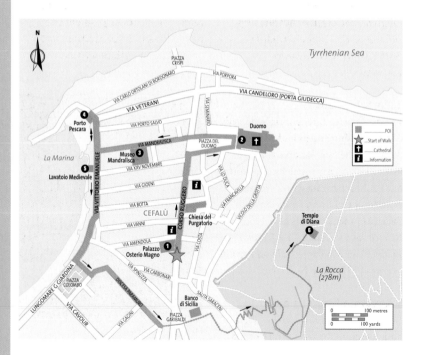

2 Duomo

The superb mosaics from the 12th century are undoubtedly the highlight, particularly the massive portrait of *Christ Pantokrator* (All-powerful Christ). Stop for a coffee or cold drink at one of the outdoor cafés and savour the atmosphere for a while.

Keeping right as you come back into Piazza del Duomo, take Via Mandralisca in front of you.

3 Museo Mandralisca

This interesting museum houses Antonello da Messina's superb *Portrait of an Unknown Man*, plus a wonderful collection of Greek pots; look for the vase with an energetically painted tuna vendor with his customer.

Continue walking downhill and turn right on to Via Vittorio Emanuele. Bear left after a few metres to Porto Pescara.

4 Porto Pescara

The picturesque little port is lined with colourful fishing boats and gives a flavour of the town's importance as a fishing port in days gone by. The Porta Marina, the city gate with a Gothic arch, was one of only four gates into the city in medieval times.

Retrace your steps along Via Vittoria Emanuele and look right, almost opposite the start of Via XXV Novembre.

5 Lavatoio Medievale

Down the steps is the restored wash house, built in the 6th century over a spring. Locals used to wash their clothes here until recent years.

From here, you can walk up to the Tempio di Diana on La Rocca. Walk south until you reach the beginning of Piazza Colombo, turn left on to Discesa Paramuro, at the end of which are steps to Piazza Garibaldi. Take the steps to the right of the Banco di Sicilia, which is the start of a clearly signposted 20-minute walk up a steep path.

If you would prefer to stay on the level, continue walking south along Via Vittorio Emanuele to the boardwalk lining the beach.

6 Tempio di Diana

Affording superb views over the town and coast, this temple from the 5th century BC shares its position with ruined Byzantine fortifications and a portal from the 9th century BC.

Open: daily 9am–7pm.

Rooftops of Cefalù

Northeast Sicily

Northeast Sicily boasts some of the most stunning scenery on the island: Mount Etna, which dominates the island physically, the characteristic villages that ring the mountain, the Aeolian Islands with their dramatic volcanic landscapes and seascapes, and the unspoiled Nebrodi mountains. The tourist mecca of Taormina with its beaches, and the vibrant city of Catania with its international airport are also to be found here.

TAORMINA

Taormina has a long history of tourism. Judging by the throngs of tourists that flood the town, and the prices of hotels, restaurants and shops, it is certainly still popular – and costly. Taormina is blessed with a stunning location on Mount Tauro, with breathtaking views over the sea and Mount Etna. It also has beaches nearby, and famously mild weather. It is therefore not surprising that it has always been a popular spot. Countless generations of the great and the good have enjoyed the superb climate here, including Goethe,

View from the stands at the Graeco-Roman theatre, Taormina

D H Lawrence, Marlene Dietrich, Tennessee Williams, Elizabeth Taylor and Francis Ford Coppola.

Taormina is perennially crowded. Restaurants and hotels are many times overbooked, prices rocket, and the town suffers from its sheer popularity. On top of hordes of resident tourists, cruise ships disgorge passengers who are bussed up the hill for daily excursions and so Taormina struggles to retain its charm and medieval character. The main street, Corso Umberto I, is filled with restaurants, high-class shops, souvenir stands, and cafés and bars in which to stop and people-watch.

Besides the charm of the old town, there are many other attractions around. It is a good base for exploring nearby spots such as Mount Etna, Catania and the stretch of beaches at the bottom of the mountain. Bear in mind that if you use Taormina as a base, you have to deal with the traffic and the climb. Consider Taormina as a day trip from other bases such as Linguaglossa or Catania.

The origins of Taormina can be traced back to at least the 4th century BC, when the Greeks moved in after the colonial wars destroyed Naxos. It is said that the population of Naxos climbed up the mountain and set up camp in Taormina as a refuge from the tyranny of Dionysus I. The town became known as Tauromenium when under Roman control from 212 BC, and found its *raison d'être* as a holiday resort, with many consuls and patricians building their luxury villas in the town. The village flourished under the Greeks and Romans, and was the capital of the Byzantine Empire, before being destroyed by the Arabs in AD 902. It also came under the control of the French and Spanish, becoming an important centre for art and trade.

Taormina has known tourists of one kind or another ever since. The great German thinker Goethe arrived in 1787 and, from this point on, it became a magnet for painters and intellectuals from all over the continent, and their work attracted further visitors to the town. One of the best known was Baron Wilhelm von Gloeden, a 19th-century photographer. Among other subjects, he took photographs of young boys in and out of classical clothes. The pictures caused scandal and fascination in equal measure, and the town's fame grew throughout Europe.

The town itself is perched high up the mountain. The sea and railway track lie below, at the foot of Mount Tauro. The nearest train station is Taormina-Giardini, from where you can take buses heading up the precipitous slopes to Taormina town to the bus station in Via Pirandello. From here, you can take the short walk uphill to the old city entrance and the start of the main street, Corso Umberto I, which traverses the heart of the medieval town. Along the Corso and its side streets, restaurants and shops of all types cater to well-heeled travellers from all over Europe. You are likely to see wedding parties strolling around the town; the spectacular location is popular for romantic, sophisticated nuptials from Italy and beyond.

The courtyard at Palazzo Corvaja

Taormina is easily visited from other bases in the area. Regular buses and a *funivia* (cable car) connect the bottom of the mountain to Taormina.
Tourist information office. Palazzo Corvaja. Open: Mon–Sat 8.30am–2pm & 4–7pm.

Chiesa di Santa Caterina

This little church dates from the mid-17th century and is consecrated to St Catherine of Alexandria. The exterior is rather unfriendly, but the interior has an impressive wood-beamed ceiling.
Piazza Santa Caterina, off Corso Umberto I. Tel: (0942) 23 123. Open: daily 9am–8pm. Free admission.

Duomo

This is one of the most unlikely cathedrals anywhere in Sicily; it looks much more like a small defensive fortress than a religious building. Dedicated to San Nicola, it was built around 1400 in the Gothic style but modified over the centuries. The portal dates from the 17th century, and has a small rose window over it. The wooden beams on the ceiling are attractively carved in the Arabic style.
Piazza del Duomo, off Corso Umberto I. Currently closed for renovations.

Palazzo Corvaja

Originally an Arab watchtower, the current structure dates from the 15th century, and is where the Sicilian parliament first met in 1411. It contains

Taormina's pretty Piazza Nove Aprile

not only the tourist office but also the **Museo Siciliano di Arte e Tradizioni Popolari** (Museum of Art and Folk Traditions). Among the items on display are 19th-century family portraits, typical donkey carts painted in traditional style, and embroidery. *Piazza Santa Catarina on Corso Umberto I. Tel: (0942) 620 198. Museum open: Tue–Sun 9am–1pm & 6–8pm. Admission charge.*

Palazzo di Santo Stefano

Near the western end of Corso Umberto is this palace, accessed by walking around to the back. It is a striking building, with a mix of Arab and Norman styles, dating from the 12th century. Black lava stone from Mount Etna was used to build it, a suitable palace at the time for the dukes of Santo Stefano. It is now home to the Fondazione Mazzullo, and exhibits temporary displays of art and sculpture.

Corso Umberto I, 242-246. Tel: (0942) 61 0273. Opening times change constantly subject to exhibitions, so check with the tourist office. Free admission.

Parco Duchi di Cesarò

The park has stunning views over the sea and towards Mount Etna; it is a tranquil place away from the crowds in the main town and has lots of shady trees to shelter under. Designed in the 1890s by Lady Florence Trevelyan Cacciola, the park is sometimes referred to as Trevelyan Gardens or Villa Comunale. Rumour has it that Lady Florence was forced to leave Britain after a scandalous affair with the heir to the throne at the time, the future Edward VII. The gardens include several follies, whimsical towers and bird cages, as well as flowerbeds, hedges and lawns. It is a delightful place to come to picnic and cool off in the height of summer.

Via Bagnoli Croce, downhill from Corso Umberto I. Open: daily 9am–midnight (10pm in winter). Free admission.

Roman Odeon

At the back of the Chiesa di Santa Caterina lie the remains of a small Roman theatre that was found in the 19th century. The existence of a single Greek colonnade and other evidence point to the site originally being the location of a Greek temple, most likely dedicated to Aphrodite.

Behind the tourist office, on the other side of Piazza Vittorio Emanuele, next to Chiesa Santa Caterina.

Teatro Greco-Romano (Graeco-Roman Theatre)

The most photographed spot in the area is the famous Teatro Greco-Romano, and once you see the view from it towards Mount Etna and the coast, you will see why. The theatre was not built as such, but formed by excavating the rock itself. It was positioned carefully at the highest point of the town, so as to create a spectacular backdrop for the stage. The Romans partially spoiled the views when they modified it to enable gladiator fights to be held there. Standing on the stage gazing up at people in the seats is unnerving: one does not need much imagination to picture a Roman crowd baying for blood. Nowadays, the theatre is the spectacular site of the annual Taormina film festival.

Via del Teatro Greco, next to Grand Hotel Timeo. Tel: (0942) 23 220. Open: daily Apr–Sept 9am–7pm, Oct–Mar 9am–6.30pm. Admission charge.

CASTELMOLA

If you fancy some strenuous walking, the steep climb to the village of Castelmola that towers over Taormina is ideal: the trip is worth the effort. From the ruined medieval castle at the top are near-360-degree views that will take your breath away. This is the summit of Mount Tauro, and allegedly the site of an ancient acropolis called the Tauromenion. For the open-minded, sample the local *vino alle mandorle* (almond wine) in Bar Turrisi, famous for its unique interior, which boasts phallic-related décor.

3km (2 miles) northwest of Taormina. Buses go from the bus terminal at Taormina, but check times at the tourist office beforehand. Alternatively, it is a 40- to 60-minute walk from the Salita Branco steps, just off Via Cappuccini in Taormina.

Best view in the area? Looking towards Mount Etna from the Teatro Greco-Romano

Walk: Taormina

This walk takes in Taormina's most popular squares and parks and gives you a taste of the charming backstreets. The tour is best done first thing in the morning, when the sun shines on Mount Etna and before the tour buses flood in.

Start at the Palazzo Corvaja. Allow three hours (leisurely pace).

1 Palazzo Corvaja

This striking building was an Arab defence tower in the 11th century, and later the seat of the first Sicilian Parliament in 1411. It now houses the tourist office and Museum of Art and Folk Traditions.
Walk a few metres to the church opposite.

2 Chiesa Santa Caterina

This 17th-century church was constructed over the ruins of the Roman Odeon, visible around the back.
Cross the square and take the street opposite (Via Teatro Greco), following it uphill for 100m (110yds) or so to the Teatro Greco.

3 Teatro Greco-Romano (Graeco-Roman Theatre)

Enjoy the amazing views of Mount Etna that the Greeks originally wanted to emphasise. Walk around the main stage and imagine yourself as an actor in Greek times or, less happily, a gladiator fighting for his life.

Walking back downhill, turn left at Via Timeone and walk down the steps, bearing left on to Via del Ginnasio until you reach Via Bagnoli Croce. Turn right and go a few metres downhill on Via Roma before entering the gardens on your left.

4 Parco Duchi di Cesarò

Also known as Trevelyan Gardens, or Villa Communale, these gardens have superb views over Mount Etna and offer a tranquil break from the crowds.
Walk back up to the junction of Via Bagnoli Croce and Via Roma and turn left, walking west and uphill on Via Bagnoli Croce. Turn left then right, walking uphill on Via Naumachia, passing the Roman remains of the Naumachie, a massive brick wall that was once a Roman gymnasium. Once you reach Corso Umberto Primo, turn left and walk along until you reach Piazza Nove Aprile.

5 Piazza Nove Aprile

This delightful square has a terrace for admiring the stunning views and is a popular meeting point for locals and visitors alike. It is home to the churches of San Giorgio and San Giuseppe, the Torre dell'Orologio (Clock Tower) and the Wunderbar Café, once patronised by Liz Taylor and Richard Burton.

Continue along Corso Umberto Primeiro to Piazza del Duomo.

6 Piazza del Duomo

This is the heart of the town, with a Baroque fountain in the centre of the square. The Cathedral of San Nicola (the Duomo) and the Palazzo Communale (Town Hall) are both located on the piazza. This is an ideal place for a refreshing drink and a seat outside at one of the cafés.

You can either finish the tour here or proceed to the town's grandest and most famous hotel for a drink in the stately lounge. Take the alley downhill until you reach Piazza San Domenico. From here, walk into the San Domenico Palace Hotel with a confident air.

7 San Domenico Palace

Although the palace was originally a Dominican monastery from the 15th century, it was transformed into a hotel back in 1896. Now reputed to be the most famous monastery-hotel in the world, it is worth taking a look around to admire the magnificent interior and the gardens at the back (restaurant and lounge open to non-residents).

Walk: Taormina

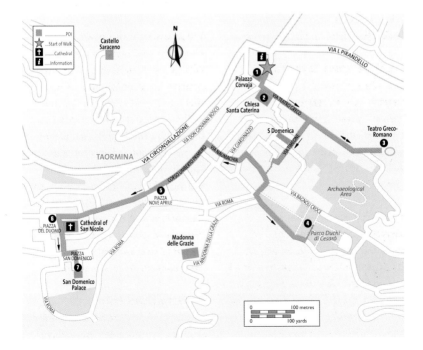

MOUNT ETNA

The importance of Mount Etna, Europe's largest active volcano, cannot be overstated – whether in terms of its symbolic power, its geographical size or its role as a tourist magnet. For many visitors, walking around and watching the mighty volcano at close quarters is the highlight of their visit to Sicily.

At 3,300m (10,827ft) high, Mount Etna towers over the eastern coast of the island, and its smoking peak is visible from most of the region. The Italian writer Leonardo Sciascia described it as a 'huge house cat, that purrs quietly and awakens every so often'. Relatively speaking, it is a young volcano, which emerged two million years ago. There have been many eruptions, including major ones in 475 BC, AD 1169, 1381 and 1669. The 1669 eruption lasted four months and destroyed most of the city of Catania.

Living on the edge: on Etna's lava-strewn slopes

Since 2004, the southeast crater has been active with violent eruptions in 2006, 2007 and in autumn 2008 when flank eruptions produced lava flows visible from afar. In April 2010, there were ash eruptions along the southeast crater's flank and an earthquake that enlarged the crater and opened fissures near Piano Provenzano.

Seismic activity stations monitor the mountain and there are webcams keeping watch 24 hours a day. Although the authorities do usually have sufficient time to evacuate the area in times of major eruptions, and even divert lava flows using excavating machinery and concrete blockades, the unpredictability of the eruptions is a constant threat.

There are several tours that can be taken to the summit and around, both during the day and at night. Day trips are ideal for getting close to the summit and seeing the action close up, which is an exhilarating experience – although for pure spectacle, watching the lava flows at night is unbeatable.

North slope

In winter, there are several ski lifts from Piano Provenzano (snow permitting), and then it is an hour's walk to the crater. In summer, 4WD vehicles make the same journey, and it is worth hiring a guide for the one- to two-hour climb from where the vehicles stop to near the crater. Check on conditions at the tourist office at Linguaglossa before undertaking this journey.

South slope

This is the more popular approach to the top, though its accessibility depends on lava flows. From Rifugio Sapienza (arrive by car or by bus from Catania via Nicolosi), tour guides and 4WD transport will take you to around the 3,000m (9,850ft) level, where you can look closely at the lava flows and the many fissures beneath the main craters. There is also a cable car up the south side of Etna, but it can be disrupted by lava flows, so it is best to check with the tourist office in Catania beforehand.

Walking to the crater from Rifugio Sapienza is an arduous three- to four-hour climb, so plan accordingly.

Train around Mount Etna

Another option is to take the private FCE train (Circumetnea), which circles Etna. From Catania, take the metro from the main train station, or a bus, to the FCE station at Via Caronda (metro stop Borgo). The train takes you around the mountain to the coastal town of Riposto, passing numerous villages and some wonderful views on the way. The trip lasts about 3$\frac{1}{2}$ hours. If you don't want to go that far, get off at Randazzo, a small medieval town that has some interesting, lava-based architecture. Riposto can also be reached by bus or train from Taormina.

Hot smoke and cold snow on Mount Etna

CATANIA

Catania has not only had to cope with being in the shadow of the island's most ominous natural feature, the mighty Mount Etna, but it has had to play second fiddle to Palermo. Until recently it suffered from heavy traffic, pollution and petty crime. However, it has come a long way in recent years. Many inner-city areas have been restored and crime has been tackled head-on, although traffic remains chaotic. Nowadays its fast-growing economy has led to the city being described as the 'Milan of the South'.

Catania has excellent transport links (including an international airport) and is a good base for exploring Mount Etna and the east of the island. It's a lively and unpretentious place, and – being a university town – is famous for its energetic nightlife. It also boasts one of Italy's grandest opera houses, where you can hear the works of the famous composer, local boy Vincenzo Bellini.

The city has experienced a roller-coaster ride in its historical fortunes since its foundation in 729 BC, when it was named Katane by the Chalcidians. It was an arch-rival of Siracusa; its citizens were sold into slavery by Dionysius of Siracusa in 403 BC. Over the next thousand years or so it was captured by the Romans, Byzantines, Saracens and Normans. The city had survived Etna's many eruptions until that of 1669; on the heels of the eruption, the earthquake of 1693 further devastated the city and surrounding countryside.

The city was rebuilt in the Baroque style by architects Giovanni Vaccarini and Stefano Ittar, who made extensive use of solidified black lava, for which Catania is called the 'city of black and white'. The city was laid out in a grid pattern, featuring spacious squares and wide avenues, so as to minimise the impact of future lava eruptions; this gave the city an elegant, airy feel that

Catania, dramatically sited below Etna

The façade of Teatro Bellini, Catania

made it one of the most admired cities in Europe.

Tourist information offices. Central Railway Station. Tel: (095) 093 7024. Open: 9am–7pm. Airport. Tel: (095) 093 7023. Open: daily 8am–9pm.
Via Vittorio Emanuele II 172. Tel: (095) 742 5573. Open: Mon–Fri 8.15am–1.15pm & 2–7.15pm, Sat 8.15am–12.15pm.

Castello Ursino

This castle was the fortress of Frederick II in the 13th century, carefully positioned on a cliff surrounded by a moat. In 1693, Mount Etna's lava reached the sea and reclaimed some coastal land, which has rendered the castle landlocked ever since. Castello Ursino is reached by walking through a pretty rough neighbourhood near the railway line and the *pescheria* (fish market). The castle's *pinacoteca* (art gallery), now the Museo Civico, has a fine collection of paintings, as well as some beautifully painted traditional Sicilian carts.

500m (550yds) southwest of Piazza del Duomo. Tel: (095) 345 830. Open: Tue–Sat 9am–1pm & 3–7pm, Sun 9am–1pm. Free admission.

Chiesa di San Nicolò all'Arena

This is Sicily's largest church, from where there are superb views over the surrounding region. Extensive renovations may prevent visitors

climbing up to the cupola, designed by Stefano Ittar. This is an impressive but stark church, begun in 1687 but never completed. Its sombre style is in complete contrast to the fanciful Baroque style of the rest of the city.
Piazza Cavour. Tel: (095) 715 9912. Open: Mon–Sat 9am–1pm. Free admission.

Duomo

Vaccarini also designed the city's cathedral in 1693, after the previous one was destroyed by the earthquake. Both the exterior and interior are typically ornate, as was the Baroque fashion, with one chapel dedicated to St Agatha, the city's patron saint. The tomb of the famous opera composer Bellini is also here.
Piazza del Duomo, Via Vittorio Emanuele II 163. Tel: (095) 320 044. Open: daily 10.30am–noon & 4–5.30pm. Free admission.

Museo Storico dello Sbarco in Sicilia 1943

This is a historical museum commemorating the Allied invasion of Sicily in 1943 and displays reconstructions of a typical Sicilian piazza and a German bunker, collections of photographs, weapons and objects, plus detailed analyses of Operation Husky.
Zō Centro Culturale, Piazzale Asia. Tel: (095) 533 540. Open: Tue–Sun 9.30am–12.30pm, Tue & Thur 9.30am–12.30pm & 3–5pm. Admission charge.

Piazza del Duomo

The heart of the city is this spacious square, surrounded by cafés, shops and historic buildings. It is a good point of reference, as the two main streets, Via Etnea and Via Vittorio Emanuele II, converge here. Via Etnea, heading north, is a wide boulevard, the main shopping street in the city, while Via Vittorio Emanuele II, crossing the city east–west, is a grimy, traffic-filled street with a number of historical sights dotted along it. At the centre of the square is the Fontana del Elefante (Elephant Fountain), designed by Vaccarini in 1736: a Roman lava-stone elephant bearing an Egyptian obelisk, topped with the insignia of St Agatha, the city's patron saint. The northern side of the square is dominated by the Palazzo del Municipio (Town Hall), another Vaccarini design.

Piscuria (or Pescheria, Fish market)

Experience Sicily's cultural patrimony first-hand at Catania's fish market, where fishermen bring in their varied catch – from catfish to crustaceans – at dawn and personally sell it. Listen to the market calls of ages past while sampling fresh bivalves and salted anchovies with a glass of passito.
Down the steps to the south of Piazza del Duomo. Open: Mon–Sat mornings.

Roman amphitheatre

In Piazza Stesicoro the remains of the 2nd-century-AD Roman amphitheatre happily coexist with 21st-century crowds and traffic. What is visible is only the tip of the iceberg: the enormous amphitheatre built of lava seated 16,000 spectators. It had fallen into decline by AD 500 and from then on its sturdy building blocks were pilfered and used to construct buildings throughout the city.

Piazza Stesicoro, Via Etnea. Tel: (095) 747 2268. Open: Mon–Sat 9am–1.30pm & 3.30–6.30pm. Free admission.

Roman theatre

These are remains of a substantial Roman theatre from the 2nd century AD and a rehearsal theatre (the Odeon) next door. It seated 7,000 people. Limestone blocks were taken from here to help build the cathedral during the 11th century.

Via Vittorio Emanuele 260. Tel: (095) 715 0508. Open: Tue–Sun 9am–1pm & 2.30–7pm. Admission charge.

Sant'Agata al Carcere

The church, built in the 1300s and dedicated to St Agatha at the Prisons, was constructed on the site of the Roman prison where Agatha was held prior to being martyred. Embedded in the Baroque façade is a 13th-century doorway with grotesques that came from the ruins of Catania's original cathedral. Inside, towards the altar, a small doorway leads to Agatha's 3rd-century-AD cell.

Piazza Stesicoro, behind the Roman amphitheatre. Tel: (095) 41 5941. Open: daily 9am–1.30pm.

The remains of the Roman amphitheatre

MESSINA

For many visitors from mainland Italy, this is a point of arrival in Sicily, just a short hop (5 km/3 miles) across the Straits of Messina. Despite the promising beauty of the harbour, this modern industrial city and port is not aesthetically pleasing. It has suffered a few disasters and was let down by the lack of vision of subsequent architects.

Messina was founded in 628 BC by the Siculans, and grew prosperous through trade between the eastern and western Mediterranean. It had significant communities of Arabs, Jews and Armenians. It was involved in the anti-Spanish revolt in 1674, thereafter falling into decline. It has had its fair share of natural and man-made disasters throughout its history (*see box*). Messina today is a city of wide boulevards and low buildings; rebuilding guidelines following the 1908 earthquake put safety before appearance.

It is easy to orient yourself in the city, mainly because the city developed around its harbour. The main streets are Via Garibaldi, which runs parallel to the seafront, and Via I Settembre, which leads from the sea to the centre of town, the heart of which is Piazza del Duomo. Many tourists do not linger in the city itself, choosing instead to use the town's excellent transport links to travel to more attractive parts of the island. However, there are a couple of sights worth visiting in Messina.

Tourist information office. Piazza Cairoli 45. Tel: (090) 67 4236.

MESSINA'S MISFORTUNES

Messina has a name for itself throughout Sicily as a disaster area. Certainly, its history does seem littered with misfortune. It was destroyed as early as 396 BC by the invading Imiico, and then suffered at the hands of the Spanish in 1674 for taking part in the anti-Spanish revolt. In the 18th century, it was struck first by the bubonic plague, then by a huge earthquake. The Bourbons pounded Messina in 1848 during the battle for Sicily's independence; six years later, a cholera epidemic struck the city. More than 90 per cent of the city's buildings were destroyed by the 1908 earthquake, which lasted a mere 30 seconds, and Messina had to rebuild once again after the Allied bombing in World War II. The town's population was forced to flee to safety, and it became known as 'the City of Ghosts'.

Chiesa Santissima Annunziata dei Catalani

This Arab-Norman building dates from the 12th century, and was restored to its former glory following the 1908 earthquake. The statue in front of the church is of John of Austria, the admiral who beat the Turkish navy at the Battle of Lepanto in 1571. Incidentally, among those injured in the battle was the famous Spanish author Miguel de Cervantes, who recovered from his wounds in a Messina hospital.

Piazza Catalani, just off Via Garibaldi. Open: Mon–Sat 9.30–11.30am, Sun 9–11.30am. Free admission.

Duomo

Although this cathedral has undergone several reconstructions, it still retains its medieval style. It contains the largest astronomical clock in the world, built in 1933, housed in the huge, 60m- (197ft-) high campanile (bell tower). Originally built in 1197 by Henry VI Hohenstaufen, it has a superb statue of John the Baptist by Antonello Gagini from the 16th century. The treasury is also worth visiting for its candlesticks, chalices and a 17th-century cloak used to cover the Madonna della Lettera.
Piazza del Duomo. Tel: (090) 774 895.
Open: Mon–Fri 7am–7pm.
Free admission.

Fontana di Orione (Orion Fountain)

This elaborate 15th-century fountain is a typically Baroque piece, designed by Giovanni Angelo Montorsoli after the construction of the city's first aqueduct, which also supplied the fountain with water. The figures that adorn it represent the rivers Tiber, Nile, Ebro and Camaro (the latter supplies the fountain's water).
Faces the Duomo.

Museo Regionale

This museum is well worth visiting if you have some time in Messina. It mostly contains works salvaged after the 1908 earthquake. These include a polyptych by the great Antonello da Messina, and two masterpieces by Caravaggio. Perhaps the most famous work is displayed in the entrance hall: 12 exquisite bronze panels depicting the Legend of the Sacred Letter, dating from the 18th century.
Viale della Libertà 465, very near Piazza dell'Unità d'Italia. Tel: (090) 361 292. Open: Mon & Fri 9am–10.30pm, Tue, Thur & Sat 9am–1.30pm & 4–6.30pm, Sun 9am–12.30pm. Admission charge.

Orion Fountain and Torre dell'Orologio

AEOLIAN ISLANDS

One of the most popular summer resorts in Sicily, this is a volcanic archipelago of seven islands. The superb summer weather, crystal-clear waters and picture-postcard scenery all add up to an irresistible draw for thousands of visitors. The scenery here is extraordinary, featuring dramatic rock formations, cliffs and volcanoes. The islands also provide excellent snorkelling, scuba diving and beaches composed of hot black sand and rocky outcrops. The volcanoes themselves offer spectacular night-time fireworks, the occasional lava display and the chance to walk to the top of a crater and peer into the fumes.

Lipari, at 36sq km (14sq miles), is the largest island with the most tourist facilities and sights. Stromboli is the most distant and volcanically active, and Vulcano, with its brooding crater and therapeutic mud baths, is the closest island to Sicily. The remaining islands (Panarea, Salina, Alicudi and Filicudi) also offer good tourist facilities and are popular with a beautiful young set and rich Italians who keep holiday villas there.

In the winter, the isolation of the islands becomes all too apparent, as vicious winds and storms batter the archipelago and ferry services are suspended. When seen in these months, it is easy to understand why the ancient Greeks named the islands after Aeolus, god of the winds. The islands' isolation and lack of natural resources have taken their toll, with many of the inhabitants choosing to emigrate – chiefly to Australia – during the last century. Even now, the islands remain sparsely populated, although booming tourism has benefited the inhabitants economically.

The Aeolian Islands are said to have been inhabited for more than 3,000 years, in spite of the volcanic activity that has continuously threatened the inhabitants. Although the volcanoes are at the end of their life cycle, even now, minor outpourings of molten lava, clouds of sulphuric gases, and red-hot jets of gas and rock illuminate the night sky, especially from the main crater at Stromboli.

There is a frequent ferry and hydrofoil service from Palermo and Milazzo on the Sicilian mainland.

THE ISLANDS AND THE SILVER SCREEN

The dramatic scenery of the Aeolian Islands provides an ideal backdrop for films, and the islands have featured in many well-known movies. Stromboli achieved notoriety in 1950 with the release of the Roberto Rossellini film of the same name starring Ingrid Bergman; the public were scandalised by the couple's off-screen affair. Stromboli was used in the film version of the Jules Verne novel *Journey to the Centre of the Earth*, starring James Mason. The water chute in Lipari's Cave di Pomice featured in the Taviani brothers' film *Kaos*, based on the short stories of Luigi Pirandello. Salina, one of the smallest islands, was used as the setting for the hugely popular *Il Postino*, which won the Best Foreign Film Academy Award in 1996.

In the summer, the islands can be reached from Cefalù and Messina too.

Lipari

The most developed of the Aeolian Islands, Lipari has good tourist facilities and is an ideal base from which to explore the other islands. Lipari's history mirrors that of Sicily to a great extent. The island's golden years were under the Normans, when the trade in volcanic by-products – pumice, sulphur and obsidian, a glass-like rock – paid dividends. In 1544, the town was sacked by the pirate Barbarossa (Redbeard), and the town's citadel was built thereafter. The island is still known for the mining of pumice stone, which you will see on sale in souvenir shops.

The only real town on the island bears the same name, and has two ports used by ferries and hydrofoils, Marina Lunga and Marina Corta. They are located on either side of the cliff-top citadel, which contains the few cultural sights on the island, the most important being the Aeolian Archaeological Museum. The main street is Corso Vittorio Emanuele, which runs vertically down the town, and contains banks, restaurants, bars and shops, as well as the tourist office.

The walls surrounding Lipari Old Town

A ferry on its way to Lipari Island

There are also four villages on the island, the main one being Canneto, just north of Lipari Town, which has some hotels and restaurants. Outside the village is probably the best beach on Lipari, Spiaggia Bianca (White Beach).

Canneto

The best beaches on the island can be found around this village, just 2km (1¼ miles) north of Lipari Town. Buses head here in their journey around the island, leaving Lipari Town from the dock at Marina Lunga. You can also hire bicycles or mopeds to explore the island. Just north of Canneto is Spiaggia Bianca, the best beach on the island. The name refers to the white pumice dust that once covered the beach. The sand is in fact a dark shade of grey, similar to the black volcanic sand common around the Aeolian Islands.

Just nearby is a series of pumice quarries, most of which are abandoned.

There are remnants of black obsidian rock and white powder around the picturesque bay of Cave di Pomice at Campobianco. Kids especially will enjoy this place, as you can slide down the pumice chutes into the sea, and cover yourself in the fine white pumice dust. Also recommended is Puntazze, on the north coast of Lipari Island very near Acquacalda, which has stunning views across to the other Aeolian Islands. Another popular spot for views is Quattro Occhi (Four Eyes), in the west of the island, which was mentioned in *The Odyssey*. The top of the hill has superb panoramas over the *faraglioni* (rocks sticking up from the water), with Vulcano in the background.

The Citadel

The castle and walls surrounding Lipari Town's Citadel (also known as Upper Town) date from the occupation of the island by the Spaniards. Via Garibaldi, which runs almost parallel to Via Vittorio Emanuele, leads to Via del Concordato, an impressive series of long steps that leads up to the Baroque Cattedrale di San Bartolomeo. This 17th-century cathedral includes a 12th-century Benedictine cloister, while the highlight inside is the silver statue of St Bartholomew, dating from 1728. Around this area, remains have been found of settlements dating back to 1700 BC, and there is a working archaeological site in the southern half of the citadel.

**Museo Archeologico Eoliano
(Aeolian Archaeological Museum)**
Worth visiting if you have time is the
Museo Archeologico Eoliano, one of
southern Italy's most complete
archaeological museums. The museum
is split into two separate buildings,
100m (110yds) or so apart. The first
covers the Neolithic and Bronze Ages
and is housed in Palazzo Vescovile
(Bishop's Palace), just south of the
cathedral. The second building is north
of the cathedral. It is known as the
Sezione Classica (Classical Section) and
focuses on discoveries from the island's
11th-century-BC necropolis. One of the
highlights of this section is the huge
array of theatrical masks, giving a

fascinating picture of cultural life and
the richness of Greek drama at the time.
*Via del Castello. Tel: (090) 988 0174.
Open: Mon–Sat 9am–1.30pm &
3–7.30pm, Sun 9am–1.30pm.
Admission charge.*

Vulcano
Vulcano is the nearest island to
mainland Sicily, and all ferries linking
Lipari with the mainland stop here. It is
extremely popular as a day trip from
Lipari. Visitors are attracted not only by
its superb black sandy beaches, but also
by its volcanoes.

Most visitors to Vulcano come to see
the Gran Cratere, which is less than an
hour's undemanding climb from the

The mud baths on Vulcano Island

Statue and rock formations, Vulcano

the most visitors. It has not erupted since 1890, however, and the crater itself seems fairly dormant. The walk up to the 418m (1,371ft) peak takes just 40–60 minutes from the ticket office near the base, and relatively easy. You can walk all around the crater, past the fizzing pools of yellow sulphur with their billowing, smelly smoke. The views from the top across to the other Aeolian Islands are awe-inspiring, and you may find yourself taking more photos than strictly necessary.

At the dock, follow the signs for 'Al Cratere', which takes you south along Via Provinciale. After 5–10 minutes, you will see a signposted gravel track on your left that takes you to a little hut that sells tickets. Remember to wear sturdy shoes and a sunhat, and take plenty of water. It is best to climb the volcano in the afternoon, when the position of the sun makes the views to the other islands more spectacular.

base, while the less energetic wallow in the Piano delle Fumarole, the sulphuric mud baths near the jetty. Vulcano's thermal bath resort is also popular, renowned for its curative powers for health problems such as rheumatism.

The island is aptly named after the Roman god of fire (Vulcan). Homer described it as the blacksmith's workshop of Hephaistos, the Greek god of fire. The English word 'volcano' in fact comes from the name of this island. Thermessa, as the island was originally called, was said by the ancient people to be the gateway to Hades (hell). When you see the sulphuric fumes belching from the Vulcano della Fosse, you will understand why they were in awe of the island.

Gran Cratere (Big Crater)

The Big Crater, the only active crater out of the four on the island, receives

Mud baths

Worth a visit, especially after the crater climb, is the Laghetto di Fanghi (mud pool). There is one large mud pit of warm, sulphurous liquid for bathing in; it is said to have therapeutic properties. The stink of sulphur and slime can make you question this, however. Don't get any mud in your eyes, as it can sting, and don't stay longer than 20 minutes. Afterwards, you can rinse off by walking into the rocky sea a few metres away, but the smell of the sulphur will certainly linger for a good few hours afterwards. Volcanic hot jets of gas bubble up from the sea, making a natural jacuzzi. Watch out where you put your feet, though, as the base of the gas jets is very hot.

A couple of minutes' walk from the dock, bearing right, at the bottom of a faraglione *(stone column). Open: 6.30am–8.30pm. Admission charge.*

Stromboli

This island is a popular boat excursion from Lipari, mainly because of its active volcano, which occupies virtually the whole island, and which can be seen in action most spectacularly at night. During the day, there are regular excursions from the village of Piscita to climb the 90-odd metres (295ft) to the top and peer down at the bubbling sulphuric stench in the crater. When the volcano spews lava, it flows down the *sciara del fuoco* (trail of fire), resulting in loud hisses as it reaches the sea, a natural event that has occurred for at least 2,000 years.

Of all the Sicilian islands, Stromboli is the furthest away from the mainland, a couple of hours by boat from Lipari Town. This isolation, as well as the volcanic activity (which has caused the inhabitants to be evacuated a number of times), explains why relatively few people live here. The village of Ginostra is on the southwestern shore, while the other main village and landing point is Scari.

Menacing Stromboli Island

Central Sicily

For the purposes of this book, Central Sicily comprises the band of land from Sciacca on the southwest coast going towards – but not including – Catania on the eastern coast. Some visitors to Sicily keep to the coastlines of the island, but there are many sights in the interior that should not be missed, including Agrigento, the stunning Roman mosaics at Villa Romana del Casale, the historic city of Enna in the centre of the island and the ceramic centre of Caltagirone.

AGRIGENTO AREA

Agrigento

Most tour buses do not stay in Agrigento town itself, focusing instead on the Valley of the Temples. This is a shame, as the town has some charm. The medieval quarter shows Arab and Norman influences, with elegant Arab courtyards and narrow passageways. The main street is Via Atenea, lined with shops, and popular for an evening stroll. Most of the sights to see are west of Piazzale Aldo Moro, a pleasant square filled with trees and cafés.
Tourist information office. Piazza Aldo Moro. Tel: (0922) 20 454.

Chiesa di Santa Maria dei Greci (St Mary of the Greeks)

The 11th-century church of Saint Mary of the Greeks was used in Norman times by Greek clergy, hence its name. It was built on the site of a 5th-century Doric Temple to Athene, the remains of which are still visible. The peaceful garden is perhaps the highlight.

At the western end of Via Atenea.
Open: daily 8am–noon & 3–6pm.
Free admission.

Duomo

This imposing building looks peculiar, with an uncompleted bell tower dating from the 15th century sitting uneasily with the rest of the cathedral, which was originally built in AD 1000. The interior is much more gracious. The wooden ceiling is beautifully painted; it dates from the 17th century. Another highlight is the incredible acoustics, best appreciated if you stand under the apse. Also worth noting are the Norman windows, which survived the reconstruction of the building in the 13th, 14th and then the 17th centuries. The cathedral is dedicated to San Gerlando, the town's first archbishop in Norman times, who is buried here.
Piazza Don Minzoni. Tel: (0922) 49 0011, at the top of the hill above the town. You can climb northwards from Piazza Pirandello or from Piazza Lena.

Open: daily 9.30am–12.30pm & 4.30–6.30pm. Free admission.

Casa di Pirandello (Pirandello's House)

Casa di Pirandello is the former home of the great Sicilian writer. Agrigento's most celebrated son was the 1934 Nobel Prize winner for literature, Luigi Pirandello (*see p25*). His most famous works include his novel *The Late Mattia Pascal*, and the plays *Six Characters in Search of an Author* and *Enrico IV*. This country farmhouse is now a museum of memorabilia from the playwright's life. His tomb lies under his favourite pine tree, where he used to sit and meditate. *Contrada Caos, Frazione (village of)*

Caos, 8km (5 miles) west of the Temple Zone, near Villaseta. Catch bus 1 from Piazza Marconi, Agrigento. Tel: (0922) 511 826. Open: daily 9am–1pm & 2–7pm. Admission charge.

Valley of the Temples

The Valley of the Temples is a 'must-see' for all visitors to Sicily (*see walk on pp113–14*). It is a UNESCO World Heritage Site and one of the most important sets of ruins on Sicily. It is crowded with tour buses all year round, and it gets very hot, so be sure to take water and a sun hat.

The Valley of the Temples was once the city of Akragas, settled by the Greeks in 581 BC. It was ruled by tyrants such

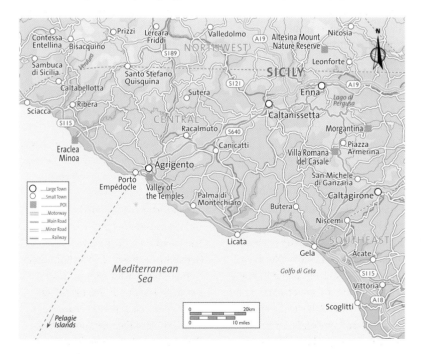

as Phalaris, who oversaw a period of economic growth that made it the richest city in Sicily. The philosopher Empedocles helped write a democratic constitution for the city, one of the first.

Akragas's Carthaginian enemies arrived in 406 BC, partially destroying the city before being ejected by an army from Corinth about 20 years later. Most of the temples date from around the 5th and 6th centuries BC. The Romans renamed the city Agrigentum in 210 BC, and built up the city's trading status; this continued under the Byzantines.

Dramatically, the city was abandoned in the 7th century under the threat of Saracen invasion, and most of the population moved up to a more suitably defensive location on top of the hill, which is now the modern city of Agrigento. This was not enough to hold the Arabs at bay. They conquered the town in the early 9th century, calling it Girgenti. After 200 years of Arab rule, the Normans came, building many of the city's now famous churches, including the cathedral.

In the 20th century, the city's boundaries spilled over into the valley below. Unfortunately, this is still a major problem, and the valley is littered with incomplete structures.

While it is still a stunning scene, the temples are in various states of ruin, having suffered from earthquakes and vandalism over the years. The best preserved is the Temple of Concord. The ruins are divided into the Eastern and Western Zones, separated by the SS 118

main road and the car park, around which are located the ticket office, café and shop. The Archaeological Museum is worth a visit too.

6.5km (4 miles) from Agrigento.

Eastern Zone

This zone consists of three temples running uphill, along a path that runs parallel to the ancient city fortifications.

Temple of Hercules The oldest temple in the valley, this dates from the 6th century BC and was used by both Greeks and Romans to worship the god Hercules. It has eight standing columns, which were put back in place in 1924.

Temple of Concord This is the undoubted highlight of the valley, and one of the best-preserved Greek temples in the world. The secret of its longevity lies in the fact that it was converted into a Christian church in the 6th century AD, which saved it from damage. The church was dismantled in 1748, although you can still see the remains of the church arches sticking out from the roof.

Temple of Juno At the end of the line of fortifications are the ruins of the Temple of Juno, which suffered an earthquake in the Middle Ages. Note the remains of a sacrificial altar near the eastern end. The red marks on the ruins are the result of fire during the Carthaginian invasion in 406 BC.

Western Zone

These ruins are not well preserved at all, although worth visiting are the Gardens of Kolymbetra, an oasis of calm.

Temple of Jupiter (Temple of Zeus)

This would have been the largest temple in the valley if it had been completed. The Carthaginian sacking of the city in 406 BC put an end to its construction, and an earthquake destroyed it completely. One of the most striking finds during excavation was a group of 38 gigantic figures of men, telamones, which would have been used to support the roof of the temple. Each one is 8m (26ft) long, and highly impressive even in their weathered state.

Temple of the Dioscuri Also known as the Temple of Castor and Pollux, there is not much to see other than four Doric columns, which were

The famous Temple of Concord, the highlight of the Valley of the Temples

reconstructed in the 19th century. Behind here is a small complex of buildings that were known as the Sanctuary of the Chtonic (Underworld) Deities, including shrines and altars.

Hellenistic-Roman Quarter

Although there is not much to see here other than ruins, it does provide a well-preserved street layout, which formed part of the city of Akragas under the Greeks, and Agrigentum under the Romans. The roads were originally laid out in the 4th century BC and form a grid of intersecting streets. The Romans added mosaic floors, as well as water storage, a heating system, and drainage for both water and sewage.

Just opposite the Archaeological Museum. Open: daily 8.30am–1 hr before sunset. Free admission.

Museo Regionale Archeologico (Archaeological Museum)

This large collection of artefacts from the excavated sites has good explanations in both Italian and English. The collection of Greek vases is impressive, as is the 8m (26ft) high telamon and a reconstructed model of a typical Greek temple. In the grounds are the 13th-century Chiesa di San Nicola and the Oratory of Phalaris, a temple from the 1st century BC.

Contrada San Nicola, on the outskirts of Agrigento on the way to the Valle dei Templi. Take bus 1, 2 or 3 from the town. Tel: (0922) 401 565. Open: Tue–Sat 9am–7pm, Sun & Mon 9am–1pm. Admission charge.

Walk: Valley of the Temples

This walk takes in the most important sights in the Valley of the Temples. The main temples are a ten-minute walk downhill from the Archaeological Museum and Hellenistic-Roman Quarter, and so are visited last to avoid a later uphill walk afterwards.

Remember to take a hat, sunglasses and water if it is a sunny day.

Allow three hours.

Take buses 1 or 3 from Piazza Marconi or bus 2 from Piazza Rosselli in Agrigento, and get off at the next stop when the bus turns left at the Hellenistic-Roman Quarter. The entrance is opposite the Archaeological Museum.

1 Hellenistic-Roman Quarter

Within the well-preserved 4th-century-BC urban plan, hunt for remains of elaborate water-storage systems, mosaic floors, mills, housing and columns. *Walk across the road to the museum, following the footpaths.*

Remains of the Temple of the Dioscuri

2 Museo Regionale Archeologico (Archaeological Museum)

This modern and well-organised museum contains a rich collection of artefacts from ancient Akragas and the temples in the area. In the same grounds are the 13th-century Chiesa di San Nicola and the Oratory of Phalaris. *Walk downhill on the Via dei Templi for 5–10 minutes, passing the car park at Piazzale dei Templi on your left, then keep right to reach the temples of Jupiter and the Dioscuri.*

3 Temples of Jupiter and the Dioscuri

The highlight of the Temple of Jupiter is the telamon lying flat on its back. About 450m (490yds) further on is the smaller Temple of the Dioscuri, also known as the Temple of Castor and Pollux, much of which is destroyed. These comprise the main ruins in the so-called 'Western Zone' of the valley. *Follow the signs to the Gardens of Kolymbetra.*

4 Gardens of Kolymbetra

Although it means paying an extra admission charge, these peaceful gardens and orchards are well worth strolling around, having been lovingly redeveloped in recent years.

Make your way back to Piazzale dei Templi and walk east along the remains of the ancient walls.

5 Temple of Hercules

Immediately inside the entrance to the so-called 'Eastern Zone' cross the ruts of an ancient road to the Temple of Hercules, said to be the oldest, dating from the 6th century BC. Only 8 of its original 38 columns are standing.

Walk uphill on the path to the Temple of Concord, which stands at the top of the hill.

6 Temple of Concord

For many, this is the highlight of the Valley of the Temples. This superbly preserved temple dates from 430 BC, and gives you some idea of how the other temples in the valley would have looked. Early Christians dug out catacombs in this area.

Continue walking east for another 400m (440yds).

7 Temple of Juno

Partially destroyed by an earthquake in the Middle Ages, the ruins of the Temple of Juno still contain traces of red, signs of fire damage from the 5th century BC.

To catch the bus back up to Agrigento, wait at the bottom of Piazzale dei Templi, opposite the café and car park.

Walk: Valley of the Temples

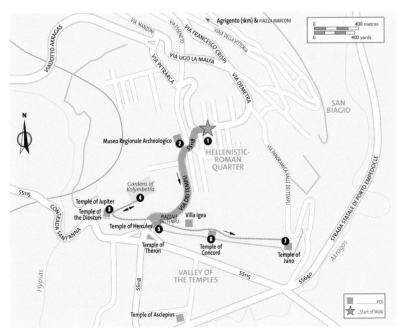

Eraclea Minoa

Myth has it that when Daedalus was kicked out of Crete, he sailed to Sicily and founded Eraclea Minoa. The small city is sited on the edge of a limestone ridge above the sea; it is nicely maintained but rarely visited by tourists. You can explore the 4th to 1st-century-BC remains of the residential neighbourhood, fortifications, temples and a tiny sandstone theatre, which has been given new life after a restoration and is used in July and August.
Open: 9am–1 hour before sunset. Admission charge.

The best beach in the area lies below the ruins and is backed by the white, limestone bluff that looks like gigantic, airy puffs of whipped cream. Well-equipped bathing establishments provide supplies; low-key bars and restaurants are hidden in the pine forest.

Sciacca

Sciacca's port is animated with fishermen and their *gozzi*, small blue-and-white fishing vessels with eyes decorating the prow. Founded by the Romans as a spa centre, locals still come for curative treatments but there is little tourist traffic. Sciacca is a centre of ceramic production as well as for salt- and oil-preserved anchovies and sardines, hence a wealth of shops offering selections of both. With no must-see monuments, a visit here is a relaxed way to get a feel for life on the island. From the port, with good fish restaurants, a staircase leads to the upper town and into Piazza Scandaliato, where you can have a *caffè* by day and listen to music by night.

Caltabellota

This sleepy hilltop village has a history of intrigue. Count Roger came through in 1090 on his way to Palermo, leaving the Chiesa Madre and a fortified castle in his wake. In 1194, William III, heir to the Norman throne, along with his mother, was imprisoned in the castle and left for dead. The peace treaty ending the War of the Vespers was signed here in 1302. The castle ruins, at almost 950m (3,100ft) above sea level, afford a spectacular 360-degree view that takes in the entire southwest coast. From the Gothic Chiesa di San Salvatore, follow the steps carved from the rock to climb to the highest point of Monte Castello and the ruins of Count Roger's castle where a single doorway still stands. Not a bad place to be at sunset.

Licata

This quiet port town with an active fishing fleet has become a destination for those coming to eat at chef Pino Cuttaia's La Madia (*see p162*). Licata also has a charming morning market, a 16th-century castle and access to beaches. On the approach to the town there are defensive bunkers constructed by the Germans in advance of the

Allied invasion of 9 July 1943. The American forces that landed here, under General Patton, were to provide flank support for British troops charged with advancing up the east coast to take Messina. Because of chaotic landing efforts complicated by rough seas and high winds, uneven Axis resistance and bickering among Allied generals, the American forces who landed near Licata actually moved west to Agrigento, quickly proceeded to take Palermo and then moved over the north coast and into Messina, General Patton famously arriving shortly before Montgomery.

The stunning beach and cliffs below Eraclea Minoa

INLAND
Caltagirone

If you had to sum up Caltagirone in one word, it would be 'ceramics'. Shop windows, frontages and balconies in this town are full of brightly painted ceramics, which have been produced here for a thousand years using the extensive clay deposits in the area. Caltagirone has long been used as a source of tiles, kitchenware and other products for wealthy families and churches all over Sicily.

Like many towns in the area, it was destroyed by the earthquake in 1693, and rebuilt in the Baroque style.

Via Roma, the city's main thoroughfare, runs to the well-known stairway of Santa Maria del Monte. This originally connected the old city above –

Santa Maria del Monte stairway, Caltagirone

the seat of the religious authority – with the new one below, where most of the government offices were located.
Tourist information office. Piazza Umberto. Tel: (0933) 53 809. Open: Mon–Fri 8am–2pm & Wed 2.30–6.30pm.

Giardino della Villa

These public gardens, designed by the architect Giovanni Battista Basile in the mid-1800s, are a delight. Shaded pathways and secluded spaces are dotted with elegant ceramic ornamentation, statues and fountains. The highlight is the beautiful bandstand in the Moorish style.
Off Via Roma, near Piazza Umberto I.

Museo della Ceramica

The Ceramics Museum traces the history of the local ceramic industry from prehistoric times to the early 1900s, with some fascinating pieces illustrating the influences of the town's various colonisers.
Via Roma, Giardini Pubblici. Tel: (0933) 58 423. Open: daily 9am–6.30pm. Admission charge.

Stairway of Santa Maria del Monte

This long flight of 142 steps is perhaps the most famous of the town's sights. The stairs are decorated with multicoloured tiles featuring geometric designs and depictions of animals, reflecting its mix of Arab, Norman and Spanish influences – among others in the town's history. They lead up to the former town cathedral, Santa Maria del Monte. The stairs date from 1608, linking the religious core of the town (the cathedral) to the civic core, the Palazzo Senatorio (Senatorial Palace). In late July every year, the stairs become the focus of festivities celebrating the nights of San Giacomo (St James), when thousands of oil lamps are placed on the stairs to create colourful patterns and lighting effects.

At the northwestern end of the town, just beyond Piazza Municipio.

Villa Romana del Casale

The Roman mosaics at Villa Romana del Casale are some of the most extensive and beautiful in the whole of Italy, if not Europe.

This wonderful villa is one of the jewels of Sicilian heritage, and one of the few surviving examples of Roman art and architecture. The fact that such a large area of mosaic-work – more than 3,500sq m (38,000sq ft) – has been so well preserved is thanks to a mudslide in the 12th century, which protected the precious floors from theft, vandalism and further destruction. It was only in 1881 that the site was discovered, and excavations have been continuing ever since.

The villa was part of a large estate from the 3rd or 4th century AD, owned by an important Roman dignitary, possibly co-emperor Maximilian. The villa is extensive in size, with 40 rooms, including baths, a gymnasium, dining rooms and gardens. There is not much left of the building itself, and there is a protective glass structure over most of the ruins, making it difficult to imagine how the villa would have looked. However, the mosaics are the star of the show, and you can walk along specially constructed walkways that give you a good appreciation of the workmanship involved and their beauty. Many of the scenes depicted are mythological, related to the purpose of the room; for example, the *frigidarium* (cold bath room) shows mythical sea creatures, while the circus hall depicts a chariot race. Since this was originally a hunting lodge, many of the mosaic scenes involve wild-game hunting.

30km (8½ miles) northwest of Caltagirone.

The main rooms

It is well worth getting hold of a plan of the villa, so that you can appreciate the layout of the building. The villa is made up of four connected groups of buildings, set around a peristyle (central courtyard).

The main entrance leads you through a triumphal arch into the atrium (forecourt). Straight ahead would have been the *thermae* (baths), including a sauna, cold room and latrines. This area would have supplied water to the rest of the house, and allowed steam to circulate, heating the house.

To the right of the main entrance, the peristyle is where the host would have greeted his guests, with gardens set

One of the superb mosaics at Villa Romana del Casale

around a central fountain. The gymnasium was also known as the Salone del Circo: mosaics here depict a chariot race in Rome's Circus Maximus. At the other side of the courtyard is a 60m-(197ft-) long corridor, which is home to some of the finest mosaics in the villa. It is known as the Ambulacro della Grande Caccia (Corridor of the Great Hunt). The main scene depicts captured wild animals of all kinds – ostriches, rhino and tigers among others – being herded on to ships bound for Rome.

To the right of the courtyard looking from the main entrance is one of the most famous of the rooms, the Sala delle Dieci Ragazze (The Room of the Ten Girls), which shows young women playing games in two-piece outfits, an extraordinary insight into female fashion of the time. One of the final rooms is the Cubicolo della Scene Erotica, which features a steamy clinch between a breathless young man and a nubile young lady.

Tel: (334) 265 7640. Open: daily 8am–30 minutes before sunset. Admission charge.

Morgantina

Not far from the Villa Romana lie the remains of the indigenous city of

Morgantina, which reached its height under the Greeks and slowly waned under the Romans. The extensive site includes some well-preserved and easily identifiable ruins. Coming into the site through the north stoa (loggia), enter the upper agora, which was bordered by stoa on three sides and, on the fourth, by the staircase leading down to the lower agora. Extensive remains can be explored: the granary, the Sanctuary of Demeter and Persephone with two round altars, a public fountain with a double basin, kilns for firing terracota and the small theatre. Behind the theatre lies the residential area where mosaic flooring survives in many of the homes.

Open: 8.30am–1 hour before sunset. Admission charge.

View over the Agora, or Roman Forum, at Morgantina near Villa Romana del Casale

ENNA

Enna has some splendid historical buildings to admire and stunning views over the surrounding valleys. It is the capital of one of the poorest regions in Sicily, with some unsightly modern urban sprawl around its slopes. However, its climate is superb, even in the summer, when the mountain air offsets the effects of the burning sun. Fog sometimes obscures the spectacular views, giving the city a spooky feel. At 930m (3,058ft) high, it is Italy's highest provincial capital and the only one in Sicily that has no access to the sea.

Enna's position at the top of a ridge with views over a wide spread of the countryside has always made it a very important city from a military point of view. It has been referred to throughout its history as *ombelico* (belly button) and *belvedere* (viewpoint). Enna is one of the few Sicilian cities not to have been founded by foreign colonists. The Siculi people, an indigenous group after whom the island was named, settled here as far back as 1200 BC, so it is one of the oldest cities in Sicily.

Enna was under Greek influence for about 500 years before it was taken by the Roman army after a two-year siege in the 1st century BC. The Arabs managed to outwit the city's mighty defences by crawling in single file through a sewer. The Arab name for the city, Kasr Janna, was corrupted by the Normans to Castrogiovanni, a name which stuck for almost 900 years, before Mussolini ordered it to be

changed back to Enna. Nowadays, the town is an important agricultural centre due to the region's fertile soil.

The main street is the pedestrianised Via Roma, a very pleasant street in the heart of the medieval city, where locals take their beloved evening *passeggiata* (stroll). Most of the town's sights are off this street, at one end of which is the Castello di Lombardia.

Tourist information office. Via Roma 413. Tel: (0935) 52 8288. Open: Mon–Sat 9am–1pm & 3.30–6.30pm.

Castello di Lombardia (Lombard Castle)

This is one of the grandest castles on the island, and it dominates the city. It was built by the Arabs and extended by the Normans. In the 13th century, Frederick II of Aragon ordered 20 towers be built around the castle walls, but only 6 have stood the test of time. There is a set of curious courtyards: one is used as an outdoor theatre. Visitors can climb the Torre Pisana, the highest tower, to appreciate the breathtaking views. You can even see Mount Etna in the distance.

Piazza Mazzini. Open: daily 9am–8pm. Free admission.

Duomo

This is an unusual building for a cathedral. Its square front is reached by a long set of attractively curved steps. The Baroque, tufa-stone façade dates from the 16th century and covers the original Gothic church, dating from

The 'Crown of the Virgin' in the Museo Alessi

1307, which was destroyed by fire in the 15th century. The interior is vast and decorated in the Baroque style. Items of note include the impressive 16th-century doorway, five paintings by Filippo Paladino and one by Borremans. *Via Roma. Open: daily 9am–noon & 4–7pm. Free admission.*

Museo Alessi (Alessi Museum)

Although this museum has a variety of artefacts on display, including an art gallery, it is the Cathedral Treasury that wows visitors. It has many stunning examples of Renaissance jewellery, including the gold 'Crown of the Virgin', decorated with precious stones and dating from 1653. The coin collection is worth seeking out, as it includes some from the Sicel-Punic era.

Via Roma 465. Tel: (093) 550 1365. Open: Tue–Sun 9am–8pm. Admission charge.

Piazza Crispi

The fountain in this square features a bronze reproduction of Bernini's famous sculpture *The Rape of Persephone*. Persephone was the daughter of Demeter, goddess of grain, whose cult was very influential throughout the Greek world. Legend has it that Persephone was abducted by Hades while gathering wild flowers in the fields below Enna and taken to the Underworld at Lago di Pergusa, 9km (5½ miles) south of town. There are remains of a small temple dedicated to Demeter just north of the Castello di Lombardia.

Southeast Sicily

The Saracen Val di Noto is marked as the provinces Ragusa and Siracusa on the modern map. Inland villages, a pleasure to visit for both their easy-going ambience and historical significance, are terraced into the bluffs of deep canyons. The splendid coastline, once lined with tuna fisheries, provides beach-going opportunities. Historical foodways are being interpreted in this region by the most concentrated grouping of knowledgeable and creative chefs on the island.

The southeast corner of the island is very different from the rest of Sicily. Here the soil is red, a strata of white limestone supports maquis and grape vines, fields are bordered with drystone walls and the very air smells of the soil, dried wild herbs and carob trees. Cicero remarked that Syracuse knew no day without sun and, indeed, a recent study undertaken to locate sites for solar

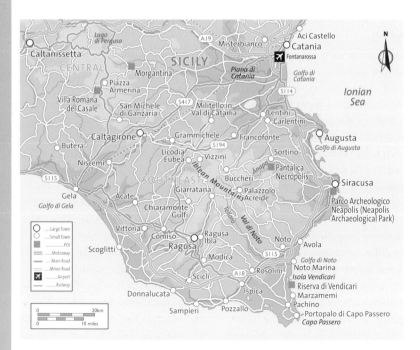

energy, recognised the area as the sunniest spot in all of Europe.

Within the Val di Noto are eight Baroque towns designated as UNESCO World Heritage Sites: Noto, Ragusa, Caltagirone, Modica, Catania, Scicli, Palazzolo Acreide and Militello in Val di Catania. All were rebuilt following the massive earthquake of 1693 and hence in the Baroque style, and all are a veritable triumph of town planning and architectural consistency. Popular beaches line the coastline: Donnalucata, Sampieri, Pozzallo, Portopaolo di Capo Passero, Vendicari. Thanks to a boom in foreign tourism and an increase in ex-pat residents (from northern Italy as well as from abroad), boutique hotels have opened all over the region.

NOTO

Leonardo Sciascia, one of Sicily's great writers, described Noto as a 'garden of stone, city of gold, city of comedy, Baroque city'. Situated on an arid plateau, Noto is one of the prettiest towns in the whole of Sicily. The picturesque countryside in this valley is resplendent with olive and almond groves, majestic carob trees, and cattle.

The history of Noto is in fact the story of two towns. Like many other towns in Sicily, Noto has seen a number of different colonisers pass through. It was known during part of its history as Neas and Netum, and was the administrative centre for one of the three provinces under Arab rule. This town's history ended on 18 January 1693, when

a massive earthquake destroyed it. There is not much left of Noto Antica (Ancient Noto), except ruins along the ridge of Monte Alveria, an eerie reminder of the bustling 17th-century town.

The new town was born 10km (6¼ miles) to the northwest, on a less vulnerable site. This massive challenge was placed in the hands of Giuseppe Lanza, Duke of Camastra, who quickly assembled a team of experts to help him. Notable among these were Rosario Gagliardi, Vincenzo Sinatra and a Flemish military engineer, Carlos de Grunenberg. This team designed a city that was at once innovative and beautifully laid out. The residential quarter of the city was located away from the political and religious quarter, while three of the main streets were laid on an east–west axis, ensuring perpetual sunshine throughout the day. The highest part of the town was reserved for the nobility and the centre for the clergy. All the buildings were constructed using soft, locally quarried limestone, the colour of which turns from white to golden as it ages.

The main street is Corso Vittorio Emanuele, now pedestrianised, which starts from Porta Reale (Royal Gate), a monumental gateway dating from the 19th century. Just beyond here is the Giardino Pubblico (Public Gardens), an ideal spot to escape the sun and crowds. It is full of palm trees and purple-flowering bougainvillaea – and of locals, too, who congregate here to socialise and start their evening stroll. Buses run from here, including those to the nearby beaches such as Noto Marina, 6km (3½ miles) away, which is perhaps the best.

Corso Vittorio Emanuele is an ideal street from which to start exploring the town, as the three main piazzas all run off here, each with their own church: Piazza Immacolata, Piazza Municipio and Piazza XVI Maggio.

Cattedrale di Noto

Dedicated to Saint Nicolas of Mira, this cathedral was built in 1776. It was designed by Gagliardi, who was a big fan of Borromini's churches and used many of the latter's designs. You cannot fail to be wowed by the extravagant sweeping staircase designed by Paolo Labisi. Tragedy struck in the winter of 1996, when the cupola and aisles collapsed. The authorities were accused

SAVING NOTO

The collapse of the cathedral's dome in 1996 was an ominous signal to the town's authorities. After centuries of decay and neglect, the monuments of Noto were now in grave danger. To complicate matters, much of the regional material – white tufa stone – is soft and does not last like marble. Unless it is constantly maintained, tufa can rapidly deteriorate. The only reason many of the buildings of Noto are still standing is because they are held up by wooden supports. Restoration is continually under way to preserve the town's glorious architecture. The town has been added to the UNESCO World Heritage Site list, which means that Noto should continue to dazzle visitors for many more years to come.

of not acting quickly enough to restore it; they had been aware of cracks caused by minor earth tremors. Luckily there were no casualties. After a long period under scaffolding, the restoration is finally complete.

Piazza Municipio. Open: daily 9am–12.30pm & 4–6.30pm.

Chiesa di San Domenico

Rosario Gagliardi's explosive Baroque façade is a masterpiece of theatricality. The elements of a classic Renaissance façade are here pushed outward and upward as if by an explosion from within. The interior is dominated by tranquil white décor with fine stucco work and attractive marble altars.

Piazza XVI Maggio. Open: daily 9am– 12.30pm & 4–6.30pm. Free admission.

Chiesa di San Francesco all'Immacolata

The austere façade of this church dominates Piazza Immacolata, contrasting oddly with the theatrical stairs leading up to it. Among the works of art here is the *Madonna & Child*, painted by Antonio Monachello in 1564, one of the many items rescued from the town after the earthquake.

Piazza Immacolata, just off Corso Vittorio Emanuele. Tel: (0931) 57 3192. Open: daily 9am–12.30 & 4–6.30pm. Free admission.

Palazzo Ducezio

Standing opposite the cathedral, this neoclassical building is now the Town

Hall. It is well worth looking inside to see the superb Salone di Rappresentanza (Hall of Representation), lavishly decorated in Louis XV style, with a superb fresco by Antonio Mazza.
Piazza Municipio. Tel: (0931) 894 592. The custodian will usually allow you to look around the ground floor during normal business hours. Free admission.

Palazzo Nicolaci di Villadorata

The palazzo is noted for its fabulous balconies which sport depictions of lions, horses, cherubs and theatrical masks. It was once the residence of a Spanish baronial family, the princes of Villadorata, but part of the building is now used as municipal offices. After a restoration programme, the palazzo has reopened. Visit the interior to understand how sumptuously the nobility of the 18th century lived. Splendid halls are richly decorated with frescoed vaults and silk wallpaper.

Balcony of the Palazzo Nicolaci di Villadorata

The building also houses a *pinacoteca* (art gallery) and the Biblioteca Comunale (town library), containing age-old manuscripts.
Via Corrado Nicolaci, just off Corso Vittorio Emanuele. Tel: (0931) 83 5005. Open: daily 10am–1.30pm & 3–7.30pm. Admission charge. Guided tours in English are also available for an extra charge.

RISERVA NATURALE DI VENDICARI

Within the reserve, wetlands and abandoned salt pans offer respite to migrating herons, egrets and flamingos. The Torre Vendìcari stands at the ruins of an old *tonnara* (tuna fishery). There is pay parking at the entrance and otherwise only a minimum of signage; trails leading to sandy coves are well worn and obvious. Bring your own supplies.
On the southeast coast, 15km (9½ miles) south of Noto.

MARZAMEMI

The fishing village grew up around the *tonnara* owned by the Villadorata family. It's a charming village with what is perhaps the most romantic piazza in all of Italy. Shops, bars, restaurants and antique shops contribute to the laid-back atmosphere of the village, from which cars are banned in summer. Come in after a day at the beach for a stroll and an *aperitivo* before dinner out in the piazza, where there is live music in summer.
20km (12½ miles) south of Noto.

RAGUSA

Although it clings dramatically to the side of a canyon, Ragusa is a fairly tranquil place, with far fewer tourists than many other Sicilian towns. It is comprised of two linked towns: Ragusa Ibla is the old town, partially destroyed by the earthquake of 1693 and rebuilt, so it is a mix of the medieval and Baroque, while Ragusa (the new, upper town) was built from scratch in the Baroque style. The two towns were merged administratively in 1927, although a friendly rivalry still exists. Unification led to many residents of Ibla 'emigrating' to the new town in search of better jobs and prospects.

Most of the sights are in Ibla, while the transport links are in the upper town. Buses run between Piazza del Popolo in Ragusa and Giardino Ibleo in Ibla. Ragusa and Ibla are separated by the so-called Valle dei Ponti (Valley of the Bridges), a deep valley that is spanned by four bridges, the most famous of which is Ponte dei Cappuccini (Bridge of the Capuchins), dating from the 18th century.

Cattedrale di San Giorgio

This is one of the best examples of Sicilian Baroque, the brainchild of Rosario Gagliardi (famous for his architecture in Noto). Started in 1738 and finished in 1775, it has an elegant façade with three tiers of columns. The neoclassical dome was added in 1820 by Carmelo Cutrano. Look out for the beautifully decorated mirror by painter Vito D'Amore, and sculptures by the Gagini School in the sacristy.
Via Roma 134, Ibla. Tel: (0932) 220 085. Open: daily 7am–noon, 4–7pm. Free admission.

The Cattedrale di San Giorgio, Ragusa

Chiesa di San Giuseppe

This church has a façade very similar to San Giorgio's, and houses precious stuccoes and paintings. Strangely, it is not certain which 18th-century architect built it, although it may well have been Gagliardi. Worth seeking out inside is the fresco work by Sebastiano Lo Monaco that decorates the cupola.
Via Torre Nuova 19, Ibla. Tel: (0932) 62 1779. Closed for renovations.

Giardino Ibleo

This beautiful public garden was laid out in the 19th century and has great views over the area. It is ideal for a rest and a spot of people-watching. In its grounds are the remains of three medieval churches; see the Gothic portal from the original Chiesa di San Giorgio with a relief of St George slaying the dragon.
At the eastern end of Ibla, just by Piazza Odierna.

Museo Archeologico Ibleo (Iblean Archaeological Museum)

One of the few sights worth seeing in the new town, the important Archaeological Museum houses finds from prehistoric times and from the Greek ruins in this province. It is divided into six sections. One of the highlights is the ancient mosaic floor from Santa Croce Camerina.
Via Natalelli by the Ponte Nuovo, off Via Roma, upper town. Tel: (0932) 62 2963. Open: daily 9am–1.30pm & 4–6.30pm. Admission charge.

A farm in Ragusa province

MODICA

Modica is a vibrant, modern city that exists within the fabric of the historic village. With its easy-going ambience and wealth of bars, restaurants and hotels, it's a great choice as a base for exploring the region.

This site, a deep canyon, has been continually inhabited since the era of the Siculi culture. It was called Motyca in the 7th century BC. During its colourful history it has rebelled against Roman rule (in 212 BC), was an important Arab city known as Mohac and was capital of the region under Peter I of Aragon. As with other towns in the region it is divided into two areas: Modica Alta (Upper Modica), which is perched higher up, and Modica Bassa (Lower Modica), built into two canyon walls and the valley floor. The two parts of town are linked by flights of stairs, notably the 250-step flight from Chiesa di San Giorgio. The maze of alleys and lanes, bordered by old shops, houses and buildings, gives a charming picture of how the town would have been in Moorish times. The other great influence on the town was 700 years of Spanish rule, which left its mark perhaps more here than on any other town in Sicily.

Modica has several claims to fame, including being the birthplace of Salvatore Quasimodo, one of Sicily's greatest writers and 1959 Nobel Prize-winner. The town contains one of the highest bridges in Europe, which at 300m (984ft) overlooks the whole town. Informative cultural tours organised by Etnos (*Tel: (0932) 753 857*) use history, poetry and music to bring the city to life.

Cartellone

This oldest of Modica's neighbourhoods and former Jewish ghetto has in the past few years undergone some subtle and slow gentrification. From here, the views over Modica are especially breathtaking at dusk, as bells toll and lights begin to come on throughout the city.
From Corso Umberto, opposite the Cattedrale di San Pietro, go through the arch and up the steps into Cartellone.

Chiesa di San Giorgio

Do not be put off by the long climb up to this church: it is definitely worth the effort. The superb tall façade is attributed to Rosario Gagliardi, and was rebuilt in 1738 after its 13th-century predecessor was destroyed by an earthquake. The majestic staircase leading up to the church is also worthy of admiration. The interior contains ten painted wooden panels depicting New Testament scenes, dating from the 16th century.
Modica Alta (upper part of town). Open: daily 9am–1pm & 3.30–7.30pm. Free admission.

San Nicolò Inferiore

Rediscovered in 1989 by a boy searching for a lost football, the rupestrian church of San Nicolò was originally built into a cave in the 11th century. Now open to the public, the space is extremely interesting as are the three layers of fresco depicting Christ and the saints popular a millennium ago.
Piazza Grimaldi, just off the Corso Umberto I at San Pietro. Open: Tue–Sun 10am–1pm & 4–7pm. Admission charge.

PALAZZOLO ACREIDE

Founded as Akrai, a colony of Siracusa, in 663 BC, the modern incarnation is a very pleasant village with Baroque churches and palaces built after the 1693 earthquake and some modern construction as a result of Allied bombings in 1943.

The citizens worship two patron saints, Paolo and Sebastiano, whose festivals are celebrated on 29 June and 10 August, respectively, in raucous (and rivalrous) fashion. Local women bake bread in honour of the saints, which is blessed and available at the church the morning of the festival. As the life-size statue of the saint exits the church and the procession begins, a wild display of fireworks and streamers fills the air with blasts, colour, smoke and occasionally flames. It's a party, but first and foremost it's a historic rite of devotion.

Akrai

Remains of once-prosperous Akrai are extremely manageable with

Looking towards Modica's cathedral

recognisable structures, delicately worked bits of stone and an intimate, 600-seat theatre with original flooring extant. A few minutes' walk from the main excavated area are the almost eerie *Santoni* (Big Saints), life-size relief statues of Demeter and her crew carved into the rock face.

1.5km (1 mile) southwest of Palazzolo Acreide. Tel: (0931) 876 602. Open: daily 9am–7pm (last admission 6.30pm). Admission charge.

Casa Museo Antonino Uccello

Anthropologist Antonino Uccello formed this ethnographic museum from his extensive private collections. On view are implements from everyday life, household objects, farm utensils, puppets and toys organised in re-created spaces to give a precise idea of what life in Sicily used to be like.

Via Machiavelli 19. Open: daily 9am–1pm & 2.30–7pm.

PANTALICA NECROPOLIS

Pantalica was settled by the Siculi in the early 1200s BC; the canyon itself is the result of the River Anapo's course through the limestone. This is Sicily's biggest necropolis with 8,000 tombs carved into the cliffs. Find good hiking through natural beauty with evidence of ancient and medieval settlements in addition to the necropoli. The park has UNESCO World Heritage status.

20km (12½ miles) northeast of Palazzolo Acreide. Always open.

SIRACUSA

For Cicero, Syracusae was 'the most grand and beautiful of all the Greek cities'. Ancient Siracusa grew from a colonial outpost into a Mediterranean powerhouse that was a match for even Athens in wealth, power and grandeur. Modern Siracusa is a typical Italian city with uncontrolled, unattractive urbal sprawl, but the historic centre on the small peninsula called Ortigia, site of the original Sicel and Greek settlements, retains its charm thanks to its isolation. The ancient city was as much as three times larger than modern Siracusa; the monuments and remains that have been excavated are mostly in the zone called Neapolis, home to the archaeological park and museum.

ARCHIMEDES, SIRACUSA'S GREATEST SON

Archimedes (287–212 BC), perhaps the greatest scientific mind in the classical world, astounded the world with his theories on geometry and mathematics. He was born in Siracusa in the 3rd century BC, returning to his native city after studying in Alexandria. Archimedes stumbled upon the principle of measuring mass through the displacement of water when he noticed that climbing into his bath caused water to slosh over the sides. He was the man who cried 'Eureka!' (I have found it!). He was also invaluable in devising ways to defend the city from its enemies, most notably when he burned the Roman fleet in 212 BC using a system of mirrors. When the Romans eventually captured the city, the order was given to spare Archimedes' life, but a Roman soldier failed to recognise him and hacked him to death in his home.

Siracusa was as important in years gone by as it is now. The history of Siracusa is rich in drama, tragedy and intrigue. The story of the city begins in 735 BC, when Corinthian settlers founded the city on the island of Ortigia, which was previously occupied by Siculian traders. A second city was established nearby on the mainland, called Acradina, on the site of the current modern city. Its early name of Syracoussai was derived from a nearby river. The city grew ever more powerful, and came to rival the great maritime powers of Carthage and Athens. A new quarter, Neapolis (New City) was created in the northwest of the city.

Siracusa flourished partly due to a rigid political structure enforced by tyrannical despot-kings, and its influence was enhanced by clever alliances. Siracusa attained such power as to provoke the wrath of Athens, which tried to capture the city in 415 BC. However, the Athenian fleet was destroyed, and the captives were imprisoned in Siracusa's notorious quarries, which are now part of the Neapolis Archaeological Park.

Siracusa enjoyed its greatest period of glory in the 4th century BC, attracting the finest minds in the Mediterranean, including Aeschylus, Pindar and Plato. When Rome emerged as a power, the city tried in vain to maintain its status through alliances. In AD 212, the city fell to the Romans under Marcellus, who looted the city and brought on a long period of decline. After the Saracens sacked the city in 878, Siracusa became little more than a provincial town, a situation that was to last for 800 years.

After the earthquake of 1693, a huge programme of restoration was undertaken in the Baroque style. The city became the provincial capital in 1865.

Ortigia

Ortigia is the Città Vecchia (Old Town), the historic heart of Siracusa. The city is undergoing restorative work to unveil new aspects of the city's beauty to the ever-increasing tourist throngs. Wandering in and out of the maze of narrow streets, and strolling around the Piazza del Duomo, is an absolute delight, by both night and day.

The Baroque façade of the Duomo in Ortigia

Duomo

Siracusa's cathedral illustrates more than any other structure in town the revolving door of foreign powers and architectural styles that have dominated the city over the centuries. The present cathedral is literally built into a 5th-century-BC Doric temple to Athena, the main structural components of which are still visible. The temple was adapted to Christian use in the 7th century AD. After the 1693 earthquake damaged the cathedral, the façade was rebuilt by Andrea Palma in the Baroque style, with dramatic statues by Marabitti. Highlights inside include a 13th-century marble font, some Norman mosaic work and statues by Antonello Gagini and his school.

Piazza del Duomo. Tel: (0931) 65 328. Open: daily 8am–6pm. Free admission.

Fontana Aretusa

On the waterfront south of the cathedral is this 1,000-year-old freshwater spring, made famous in mythology. The river god Alpheus fell in love with the sea nymph Aretusa; she became a freshwater spring to escape his attentions. Not wanting to lose her, Alpheus turned himself into a river. The spring is now ringed with papyrus and populated with ducks.

Via Picherali, near the southwest corner of Ortigia.

Palazzo Bellomo

The Palazzo Bellomo, named after the family that owned it in the 15th

century, is now home to the Regional Gallery of Medieval and Modern Art. It is an ideal museum to pop into without exhausting yourself, and it is set in an atmospheric former 13th-century monastery. Among the treasures of art and sculpture from the Middle Ages through to the 20th century are masterpieces that should not be missed: *The Burial of St Lucia* by Caravaggio, dating from the early 1600s, Antonello da Messina's *Annunciation* (1474) and the sculptures from the Gagini School on the ground floor.

Via Capodieci 16.
Tel: (0931) 69 511. Open: Tue–Sat 9am–6pm, Sun 9am–1pm.
Admission charge.

Piazza Archimede

This is a good place to get your bearings on Ortigia, as it lies right in the middle of the island. The centrepiece of the square is a delightful 20th-century fountain by Giulio Moschetti. It depicts Artemis the Huntress surrounded by sirens and handmaidens. Among the stunning old *palazzi* (mansions) that surround the square are Palazzo Platamone, now the Banca d'Italia, which has a lovely courtyard, and the recently restored Palazzo Gargallo, a 17th-century stunner in the Venetian style. This is a good place to have a coffee and admire the wonderful architecture.

In the centre of Ortigia Island, reached from the mainland via Corso Matteotti.

Piazza del Duomo

Occupying the highest part of the island, the Piazza del Duomo is where the ancient acropolis once stood. The irregular piazza is especially majestic when the façade of the cathedral is dramatically caught by the setting sun, or when it is floodlit at night. Acclaimed as one of the most beautiful squares in Italy, it is lined with fine Baroque buildings that were built post-1693. They include the striking Palazzo Beneventano del Bosco.

The Palazzo Municipale was built in 1629 by Spanish architect Juan Vermexio. In the inner courtyard is a sumptuous carriage from the 1700s. At the southern end of the piazza is Chiesa di Santa Lucia alla Badia, dedicated to the city's patron saint.

A few minutes' walk south of Piazza Archimede on Via Landolina.

Tempio di Apollo (Temple of Apollo)

Dating from the late 7th or early 6th century BC, this is thought to be the first Greek temple raised on Sicily. The Doric temple was built of sandstone with 6 x 17 columns and measured 58 x 24m (190 x 79ft). Remains include the *stylobate*, the bottom parts of columns and pieces of the *cella*. Note the inscription to Apollo on the steps on the east side.

Piazza Pancali, near the bridge to the mainland.

An aerial view of Ortigia Island

Walk: Around Ortigia Island

This tour takes in the main attractions of Ortigia Island, which can be seen in half a day. The Old Town is very compact, with little traffic, narrow streets, wide piazze and long views over the sea, making it an ideal place for a leisurely stroll.

Allow three hours. It is worth timing your walk to fit in with museum opening hours.

1 Tempio di Apollo

This was one of the first Greek buildings on Sicily. Although just a few of the Doric columns remain, one can imagine what an impressive structure it must once have been.

Turn left on to Corso Matteotti, an elegant street full of fashion shops.

2 Piazza Archimede

This lovely square sits virtually in the centre of the island and is a popular

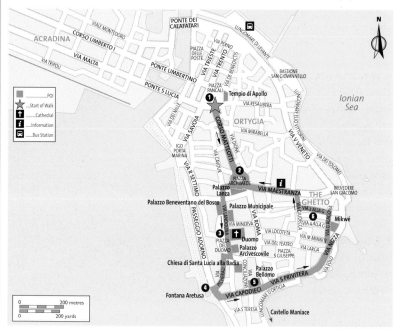

place to drink coffee and people-watch. The superb fountain is by Giulio Moschetti, depicting Artemis the Huntress. Catalan-Gothic *palazzi* surround the square.

Take Via Almalfitania heading west, then take the first left, Via Landolina, heading south. You will pass the Palazzo Beneventano del Bosco on your right and the Palazzo Municipale on your left.

3 Piazza del Duomo

Many describe this as one of the most wonderful public squares in Italy. You cannot miss the superb Baroque façade of the cathedral on your left. The building is a palimpsest of the layers of history that is Sicily. Enjoy the marvellous setting at one of the outdoor cafés facing the cathedral.

Continue south on Via Picherali, where the quaint streets lead you to the sea.

4 Fontana Aretusa

This 1,000-year-old natural freshwater spring is now populated with ducks and papyrus plants. It is a popular spot for locals to pause during their evening stroll.

Take Via Capodieci heading east, keeping an eye out for an imposing historic building on your left, at no 6.

5 Palazzo Bellomo

Palazzo Bellomo is an attractive 13th-century building, and home to the Galleria Regionale.

Continue along Via Capodieci as the name changes to Via S Privitera and Via Nizza. From Via Nizza, turn left into Via G Alagona.

6 The Ghetto

The zone of parallel streets running between Via Alagona and Via Giudecca was the Jewish ghetto from the the 6th century AD until the mid-1500s, when all remaining Jews were expelled from the city. At the corner of Via Alagona and Via 4 alla Giudecca, are the *Mikwé* (purification baths), the oldest existing Jewish baths in Europe (*Tours: 11am, 12, 4, 5, 6 & 7pm. Admission charge*).

Via 2 alla Giudecca leads to Via Giudecca; turn right and then go left on Via Maestranza to make your way back into Piazza Archimede.

Remains of the Tempio di Apollo

OUTSIDE SIRACUSA

While Ortigia Island contains the treasures of the historic centre, most ancient monuments are in the Neapolis Archaeological Park, on the outer limits of the city. Tackling this as well as the large Archaeological Museum nearby is just about manageable in one half-day, but it is probably best to set aside a whole day to enjoy both to the full.

Catacombs of San Giovanni

The Roman decree that banned the burial of Christians within the city walls forced Christians to use these former Greek underground aqueducts as burial chambers. To enter the catacombs, go into the ruined Basilica di San Giovanni, once the Cathedral of Siracusa. St Marcian, the first bishop of the city, met a cruel end here when he was flogged to death in AD 254.
Basilica di San Giovanni, Via San Sebastiano. Tel: (0931) 64 694. Open: Mar–Nov Tue–Sun 9.30am–12.30pm & 2.30–5pm. Admission charge.

Museo Archeologico Paolo Orsi (Archaeological Museum)

This ultra-modern building, set in the gardens of Villa Landolina and opened in 1988, is one of the largest and most important archaeological museums in Sicily. It was named after Paolo Orsi (1859–1935), the famous archaeologist who founded the original museum in the late 19th century.

It is divided into three sectors. Sector A gives a geological overview and covers the Palaeolithic period to early Greek civilisation, while Section B is devoted to Greek colonisation. The famous headless *Landolina Venus* is here, a Roman copy of an original by Praxiteles, which was found in Siracusa in 1806 by Saverio Landolina. Section C focuses on the Greek colonies of eastern Sicily. One of the highlights is the *Enthroned Goddess Persephone*, dating from the 6th century BC.
Viale Teocrito 66. Tel: (0931) 46 4022. Open: Tue–Sat 9am–6pm, Sun 9am–1pm. Admission charge.

Parco Archeologico Neapolis (Neapolis Archaeological Park)

Siracusa's Archaeological Park is the town's most visited site. The Parco Archeologico Neapolis is about 25 minutes' walk northwest from Ortigia Island. Alternatively, take one of the many buses from Piazza della Posta.
Tel: (0931) 65 068. Open: daily 9am–6pm. Admission charge.

Teatro Greco (Greek Theatre)

This grand theatre, with one of the largest *cavea* in the Greek world, was hewn from mountain rock during the reign of Hieron I in the 5th century BC. The theatre would have housed a capacity crowd of 16,000 and put on plays by the likes of Eurypides and Aeschylus. The theatre was much restored in the time of Hieron II in the 3rd century BC, and the Romans made further alterations in order to stage gladiatorial combats. Today Greek classical drama is performed every May and June at the theatre.

Latomia del Paradiso (Paradise Quarry)

Outside the entrance to the Greek Theatre are these infamous ancient quarries where prisoners-of-war from the Athenian invasion languished in the 5th century BC. Stones quarried here were used to build some of the great monuments of the city.

Orecchio di Dionisio (Ear of Dionysius)

At nearly 60m (197ft) long, this huge cave has extraordinary acoustics. On seeing it, the painter Caravaggio dubbed it the 'Ear of Dionysius', because he thought that the despot Dionysius must have built it so he could hear the conversations of his prisoners. It may well have been used by actors practising their lines before performing at the nearby theatre. Just a few metres away is the Grotta dei Cordari (Rope-makers' Cave); the high humidity of the cave made it ideal for shaping rope.

Ara di Ierone II (Altar of Heiron II)

It is difficult to imagine that this mammoth stone base was in fact an ancient abattoir, where 450 oxen met their end, sacrificed to the gods by teams of Greek butchers. Known as the Ara di Ierone II, only a few pillars still stand of this 3rd-century-BC sacrificial altar.

Roman Amphitheatre

This ranks as the third biggest amphitheatre in Italy, after the Colosseum in Rome and the amphitheatre in Verona. Dating from the 2nd century AD, it was used for horse races and gladiator contests. The area behind, in Viale Paolo Orsi, was used as a 'chariot park'. The Spaniards who arrived in the 16th century used the site as a quarry to build the city walls on Ortigia.

The Ear of Dionysius

Getting away from it all

For those who have had their fill of sightseeing or city life, there are many opportunities in Sicily to escape to enjoy nature, the beach or watersports. There are a number of natural parks to walk around, including the area surrounding Mount Etna, as well as many beaches and coastal sites ideal for scuba diving or snorkelling.

Beaches

In summer in particular, Sicily becomes a magnet for tourists from mainland Italy and beyond, who flock to the island to take advantage of the superb climate, crystalline waters and lovely beaches. Some of the most popular beaches are described below.

Capo d'Orlando (Tyrrhenian coast)

There are both sandy and rocky beaches here, the best being to the east of the town, which is noted for its calm and clear waters.
60km (37 ¹/2 miles) east of Cefalù, 70km (43 ¹/2 miles) west of Messina.

Golfo di Castellammare

Sandy beaches lie to the east of Castellammare, while pebble coves dot the coastline to the west all the way to San Vito lo Capo. San Vito has a bustling boardwalk and beach clubs lining its vast, sandy beach. The coves around the gulf are mostly small, open beaches with at most minimal services

(cool drinks, lounge chairs). The pristine waters and romantic coves of the Zingaro Nature Reserve are accessible only on foot via rugged paths leading down from the hiking trail.

Lido Mazzarò (Taormina)

If you want colour, and reminders of a time when celebrities lounged on the sands and cooled off in the beachside restaurants, this is the place for you – though it has the crowds and prices to match. If the tourist hordes prove suffocating, head for the beaches further north such as Isola Bella, Lido di Spisone and Baia delle Sirene.
A 15-minute cable-car ride down from Taormina and then a bus ride.

Mondello (near Palermo)

This stretch of sandy beach that extends to 2km (1¹/2 miles) becomes chaotic in the summer, when the residents of Palermo rush here to bathe in the waters and pose on the beach. There are lots of bars and restaurants along the shoreline, many specialising in good-value seafood, especially around Viale Regina Elena.

12km (7 miles) north of Palermo. Buses here leave from Piazza Gasperi to the north of the town.

Ragusa (southeast Sicily)

Perhaps the best beach in this corner of Sicily, this is an ideal place to base yourself if you are exploring the Baroque towns of Noto and Ragusa. While there is a certain tackiness about other resorts in the area, this is not evident at Ragusa. The main beach is called Marina di Ragusa, and is based around a 16th-century watchtower.

20km (12 1/2 miles) southwest of Ragusa.

Sciacca (southern coast)

The beaches on this stretch of coast are popular with Sicilians, but some of the more deserted ones are around this pretty town. Ones to recommend are San Marco and Contrada Sobareto. Another superb resort outside of Sciacca is Torre Macauda, which also has a lovely beach and good facilities.

55km (34 miles) northwest of Agrigento. Torre Macauda is 9km (5 1/2 miles) east of Sciacca.

Spiaggia Bianca (Lipari, Aeolian Islands)

Although called Spiaggia Bianca (White Beach), the powdery sand is actually greyish in colour, which makes for an unusual beach experience. It is a very pleasant spot, and is the most popular beach on Lipari Island. Alternatively, Spiaggia Sabbie Nere on Vulcano Island is worth visiting.

Just outside the village of Canneto, 3km (2 miles) north of Lipari Town. Buses from the dock at Lipari Town will take you here along the coast.

One of the deserted beaches in the Zingaro Nature Reserve

Getting away from it all

Birdwatching

The most popular areas are:

The **Saline di Trapani e Paceco Nature Reserve**, home to the famous salt pans, became a nature reserve in 1984. Sicily's largest lagoon is used by migratory birds as a stopover point, and is a fertile habitat for all kinds of plants, birds and underwater flora.

The **Lago Biviere Nature Reserve**, in the Gela area, is home to rich wildlife and plant species such as orchids and the cornflower. You can also find several duck species, and mammals such as foxes and weasels.

The LIPU (Lega Italiana Protezione Uccelli – Italian League for the Protection of Birds) oasis at the **Montallegro Lake**, Agrigento. Because the vegetation is not very dense here, it is ideal for spotting migratory birds such as cormorants and herons.

Vendicari Nature Reserve, along the south coast near Noto, is another oasis for migratory birds such as swans and flamingos. The most southerly of all of Sicily's reserves, it is comprised of several marshy areas.

Nature reserves and other green spaces

Nature is at its most dramatic and picturesque in Sicily. Because of the variety of landscapes, from rugged mountains to sandy beaches, from volcanoes to rolling hills, there is something for everyone. You do not have to travel far to enjoy a superb view of some kind.

There are plenty of opportunities for walking. The most popular nature reserves are those at Mount Etna, the Madonie Mountains and Nebrodi Mountains. In the Aeolian Islands, you can climb up the volcanoes of Stromboli and Vulcano, enabling you to see nature at its most violent and unpredictable. The views of the surrounding islands are breathtaking.

One of the few environmental successes on the island has been the increase in the number of nature parks and green spaces that have been created over the last 50 years. There are now a great number of these spread across Sicily and its islands (*www.parks.it*).

The Aeolian Islands

The best places for walking in these islands are Stromboli, Vulcano and Panarea. You could base yourself on the biggest island, Lipari, which has excellent facilities as well as the best transport links.

Vulcano, just 15 minutes by ferry from Lipari, is the easiest volcano to climb on the Aeolians. It is relatively safe, with the only unpleasantness being the smelly, sulphurous smoke that billows from sections of the crater's rim. The spectacular views towards the other islands make the journey worthwhile.

Stromboli is more remote, necessitating a two-hour boat trip from Lipari. The displays staged by the volcano at night are spectacular, though, with sparks billowing out from the crater at regular intervals. Organised guided walks to the top are available, although the strenuous climb takes approximately one hour. For a more sedate experience, you can visit the *sciara del fuoco* (trail of fire), where lava courses down a long slope to roll into the sea, to the accompaniment of steam-filled hisses.

Aeolian Islands. 1hr by ferry/hydrofoil from Milazzo. Main tourist office is at Via Vittorio Emanuele 202, Lipari Town, Lipari. Tel: (090) 988 0095.

Madonie Mountains

The island's most famous national park is the Parco Naturale Regionale delle Madonie, home to some of the highest mountains after Mount Etna, such as Pizzo Carbonara at 1,980m (6,496ft). The park is superb in both summer and winter. Skiing takes place here when there is snow, and horse-riding facilities are available. There are several towns that are ideal bases for walking in the mountains, such as Petralia Soprana and Petralia Sottana.

Black volcanic rock and erupting crater on Mount Etna

Getting away from it all

Parco delle Madonie. Driving from Cefalù, follow the directions for Santuario di Gibilmanna, 14km (8 3/4 miles) south. Tours run from the tourist office in the village of Petralia Sottana. Tel: (0921) 68 0840.

Mount Etna

The Etna Park offers skiing, horse riding and a wide choice of walks, including the Valle del Bove (Oxen Valley), a spectacular hollow, the shape of which was changed by the 1992 eruptions. Also worth visiting are Bocca Nuova and Monte Zuccolaro, popular with photographers and nature enthusiasts. The most popular hikes are to the large craters at the summit, starting from Rifugio Sapienza, Rifugio Citelli and Piano Provenzana.

Summer is the best time for hiking, as the winter months see snow and freezing conditions. Many plants have succeeded in colonising the lava soil, while poplars grow in the more humid areas. Despite centuries of hunting, there are animals too, particularly the Sicilian partridge and *Dendrocopus* (woodpecker).

Parco dell'Etna. Tel: (095) 914 588. Rifugio Sapienza is the best base for hikers.

Nebrodi Mountains

The Nebrodi Mountains make up the largest forested area in Sicily. Picturesque lakes, valleys and peaks dominate the landscape. The highest peak is Monte Soro at 1,850m (6,070ft), which becomes covered in snow like many other peaks here in the winter months. A nature reserve was established here in 1993 to protect the rich variety of wildlife, which had previously been at risk from hunters. The name comes from the Greek word *nebros* (roe deer). At the centre of the park is Lake Biviere di Cesaro, its rich marshes ideal as a meeting point for migratory birds.

Parco Naturale Regionale dei Nebrodi. Tel: (0921) 333 015.

Palermo

Some visitors can find the capital quite oppressive after a couple of days negotiating the bustling and noise-filled streets. The most attractive parks and green spaces in the city are:

Parco della Favorita, 3km (2 miles) north of the city. Palermo's biggest park, it was used as a royal hunting lodge at the time of Ferdinand III of Bourbon. Includes local fauna, tennis courts and a football stadium. (*Always open. Free admission.*)

Villa Giulia on Via Abramo Lincoln, La Kalsa district. This 18th-century landscaped oasis includes deer and a small train. (*Open: daily 8am–8pm. Free admission.*)

The **Orto Botanico** (Botanic Gardens), just next door to Villa Giulia, covers an area of 10ha (25 acres). This is a real green lung and an important sanctuary for various plant species. It also contains busts dedicated to historical figures. (*Open: May–Aug 9am–8pm, Sept 9am–7pm, Oct–Apr 9am–6pm. Admission charge.*)

Other Sicilian nature parks and reserves

Altesina Mount Nature Reserve near Enna is a major tourist attraction, situated at the bottom of a mountain. Populated by pine, eucalyptus and beech woods, it is home to a rich variety of wildlife as well as archaeological finds.

The Sicani Mountains in the south of Palermo province are home to several pretty lakes such as Lago Prizzi, as well as being an ideal habitat for migratory birds.

Monte Pellegrino Nature Reserve, also in Palermo province, is rich in biodiversity, including 25 types of orchid and half the mammal species found on the island.

Alcantara Valley, near Naxos in northeast Sicily, attracts many tourists to its eye-catching gorges formed by volcanic lava and centuries of erosion. The river of the same name is one of the most important in Sicily, gaining in size as it flows towards Mount Etna. Brave tourists flock to the gorge in the summer to bathe in the icy waters.

Vegetation around Mount Etna

Shopping

As in other Mediterranean countries, appearance is important to the Sicilians, and people tend to spend their money on high-class clothes and shoes. There are countless boutiques specialising in superb leather shoes and bags, designer clothes and lingerie. Crafts, edible items, housewares and antiques are characteristically Sicilian objects that make good souvenirs and gifts.

Handicrafts

Sicily has a wealth of handicraft products to tempt souvenir and gift-buyers. The island's rich traditions and regional specialities are reflected in the products on offer. For example, Caltagirone is famous for its ceramics, which are heavily influenced by Arab designs. Sciacca, Palermo and Santo Stefano di Camastra have their own characteristic ceramic styles. Embroidery is traditionally of a very high standard in the provinces of Ragusa and Catania, and especially in towns where convents were established around the 15th century. Erice in the west of the island is well known for its *frazzata* technique, which uses colourful geometric designs, and for hand-loomed rugs.

Also sold as souvenirs are the famous *pupi* (puppets), Sicilian marionettes used in tales that are based around legends of medieval knights. Another typical product is the *carretto* (Sicilian cart). Before the motor car, these were the major form of transport in Sicily, decorated in vibrant colours with intricately carved designs.

Look out for nicely woven baskets and brooms, items carved from olive wood and kitschy lava souvenirs from Mount Etna.

Food and drink

A huge range of fine foods can be bought in Sicily – and they make great presents. Sicily excels in citrus fruits, organic fruit preserves, nougat, almond-paste sweets and wonderful pastries such as *cannoli* and *cassata*. *Frutta di martorana* (marzipan fruits) are exquisitely made; these are available from pastry shops and confectioners.

Delicatessens and wine shops are a good source of speciality foods. High-quality wines and olive oils are also a good buy. Vegetables in oil are popular, such as black olives and aubergines, or preserved fish, such as tuna, anchovies and sardines.

Where to shop

The tourist centres are inevitably more consumer-oriented than smaller towns and villages and have a wide range of shopping options including departments stores. Palermo, Catania and affluent towns such as Taormina, Siracusa, Modica and Trapani have pricey boutiques aimed at well-heeled residents and visitors. Markets and street vendors are a good source for foods and also for expertly made crafts. Markets and antique shops sell interesting vintage items, from kitchen utensils to colourful tiles.

Most shops close for siesta, food shops usually close on Wednesday afternoons and many other shops remain closed on Monday mornings.

Palermo

Boutiques and national chain department stores are concentrated on Via Roma, Via Maqueda and along the Viale Libertà and its cross-streets. Local designers and craftsmen have their shops on Via Bara all'Olivella and Via dell'Orologio. In addition to Palermo's main food **markets** (*see p38*), there is a flea market just behind the cathedral in and around Piazza Papireto and a Sunday morning vintage market in Piazza Marina.

Roberto Intorre is a Sicilian contemporary jewellery designer working with galvanised silver, natural stones and designs abstracted from Sicilian and North African motifs. *Via Bara all'Olivella 115. Tel: (393) 476 1411.*

Shopping

Caltagirone is famous for its ceramics

At **La Coppola Storta** find a huge selection of Sicilian *coppole* (berets) in unusual materials. *Via dell'Orologio 25. Tel: (091) 743 4745.*

Paoline Libreria Multimedia is the bookshop of the Pauline sisters, one of whom has put together an extensive selection of Sicilian folk-music CDs, across the street from Palermo's cathedral. *Via Vittorio Emanuele 456. Tel: (091) 651 2158.*

The **de Simone** family of ceramicists create Sicilian ceramic designs in a modern style, sought by collectors for decades. *Via Gaetano Daita 13B. Tel: (091) 584 876.*

Peccatucci di Mamma Andrea offers a plethora of mouthwatering original creations, including preserves, sweets, honey and *frutta di Martorana. Via Principe di Scordia 67, near Piazza Florio, Vucciria. Tel: (091) 334 835.*

Enoteca Picone is the island's most well-regarded wine shop with highly knowledgeable staff; ask for Vera. *Via Marconi 36. Tel: (091) 331 300.*

The **Addio Pizzo** shop sells goods made by participating members of the anti-Mafia consortium. *Corso Vittorio Emanuele 172. Tel: (091) 976 2286.*

Northwest
Pina Parisi and her daughter, Francesca, hand-weave Erice's traditional rugs in their shop. *Via Vittorio Emanuele 21, Erice. Tel: (0923) 869 641.*

The Dainotti family make the rich, red-glazed majolica typical of Santo Stefano di Camastra that is on display

at their shop **Terre Cromate**. *Via Vittoria 107, Santo Stefano di Camastra. Tel: (0921) 337 576.*

Ceramiche Perrone is a family buiness where generations model, fire and paint figurines and accoutrements necessary for elaborate nativity scenes. Alongside the important saints, find miniature foods, animals and faithfully re-created objects of daily life. *Corso Vittorio Emanuele 106, Trapani. Tel: (0932) 29 609.*

Northeast
The shelves of **Orsola Naturalmente Sicilia** are stocked by the owner of Taormina's best restaurant, Osteria Nero d'Avola, with the fruits of his gastronomic research. *Corso Umberto 53, Taormina. Tel: (0942) 23 227.*

Le Colonne weaves Graeco-Roman motifs into modern styles to create fine contemporary jewellery. *Corso Umberto I 164, Taormina. Tel: (0942) 23 680.*

Central
Ceramica Silva crafts traditional ceramics with typical Caltagirone motifs and colours and in characteristically Sicilian forms such as the Moor's head vase. *Piazza Umberto I 19, Caltagirone. Tel: (0933) 55 707.*

Improntabarre creates ceramics in modern, thoughtful, playful designs. *Via Scala Santa Maria del Monte 5, Caltagirone. Tel: (0933) 40 538.*

Southeast

The best places in Modica for handmade chocolate and pastries are: **Dolceria Donna Elvira** *Via Risorgimento 32. Tel: (0932) 764 359.* **Antica Dolceria Bonajuto** *Corso Umberto I 159. Tel: (0932) 941 225.*

Tamì boutique in Siracusa has gathered a thoughtful selection of wine, food, books and objects of design. *Via Cavour 13, Siracusa. Tel: (0931) 465 926.*

Fratelli Bugio, in the heart of Siracusa's market, has a large selection of the best cheeses made on the island. *Piazza Cesare Battisti 4, Siracusa. Tel: (0931) 60 069. Open: mornings only.*

Paolo Mallia of **Il Rigattiere** collects, buys and sells antiques and curiosities. He has a wide collection of old ceramic serving plates, and charming quince paste moulds, for example. *Via Marzamemi 29, Marzamemi. Tel: (380) 451 7754.*

The first shop on Sicilian soil of native designer **Elio Fronterrè**. Hand-crafted clothing exalts the female form and incorporates images of iconic Sicilian motifs. *Piazza Regina Margherita 22, Marzamemi. Tel: (328) 561 4364.*

Siculamente Putia has cleverly designed T-shirts and gadgets with wry sayings in Sicilian dialect. The flagship shop is in Ragusa with outlets in tourist centres and sales via hip stores around the island. *Via Pietro Novelli, 10 Ragusa Ibla. Tel: (0932) 713 937. www.siculamente.it. Also at Piazza della Rimembranza, Pozzallo; Largo dei Vespri 1, Catania; and Via Roma 111, Cefalù.*

Stalls selling souvenirs in Taormina

Olives and olive oils

Extra-virgin olive oil

Myth gives invention of the olive tree to Athena, goddess of wisdom, who created it as a plant particularly useful to mankind. It was probably first cultivated in Sicily by the Phoenicians around the 6th century BC. Sicilian olive groves were expanded by the Greeks and fully developed by the Romans, both of which cultures used the tree for wood, the olives for food and the oil for food as well as for medicinal purposes, hygiene, illumination and as votive offerings to the gods in their pantheon.

Health benefits

Extra-virgin olive oil is one of the pillars of the Mediterranean diet as the primary fat used in the kitchen. High in vitamins A, D and E and rich in biophenols, which have antioxidant properties, extra-virgin olive oil helps reduce inflammation, retards ageing on a cellular level and prevents certain cancers; it helps prevent cardio-vascular disease by reducing the oxidation of LDL cholesterol and raising levels of HDL cholesterol.

Production

The soil and microclimates of the island are particularly well suited to olive cultivation. The evergreen trees flower in spring, producing fruit that begins to ripen by mid- to late October. Most oil-olive varieties are born green, turn purple as they mature and eventually become black. Because extra-virgin olive oil is mechanically extracted from the pulp of the olive, like a fruit juice, the integrity of the fruit is crucial. To obtain high-quality extra-virgin olive oil, olives should be carefully picked by hand and pressed as soon as possible in production facilities that are rigorously clean. To prevent oxidation and thereby retain health and organoleptic properties, extra-virgin olive oil should be filtered or, in any event, separated from sediment that forms by precipitation; it should be stored in absence of air, heat, light and metal.

Classifications

'Extra Virgin' refers to olive oils that have been mechanically, as opposed to chemically, extracted and have not begun to oxidise. DOP certification (*denominazione di origine protetta*: certified production zones) is more rigorous as the oil must also undergo a sensory evaluation. Note that there is just one pressing, and that using heat in the production process automatically produces an olive oil that cannot qualify as extra virgin. Slightly oxidised virgin olive oils are also mechanically extracted but rarely found on the market as they are almost always blended with chemically refined olive oils to make what is classified as Olive Oil.

Sicilian olive varieties

About 35 cultivars are present in Sicily, of which 8 are most diffuse: Biancolilla, Cerasuola, Moresca, Nocellara del Belice, Nocellara Etnea, Ogliarola Messinese, Santagatese and Tonda Iblea. Generally, high-quality Sicilian extra-virgin olive oils are full bodied, balance bitterness with spiciness, and present aromas of nuts and of both green and red tomato; the intensity of the aromas depends on the goal of the producer. Six DOPs are recognised in Sicily: Valli Trapanesi, Val di Mazara, Valle del Belice, Valdemone, Monte Enta and Monti Iblei.

Because most oil production comes from very small farms, there is a huge array of producers. A few to look for are: Titone, Planeta, Occhipinti, Vigo, Furgintini, Pianogrillo, Aragona, Cornellissen, Sallemi and Merlino.

Olives growing on Stromboli Island

Entertainment

Sicily's rich cultural life ensures a good choice of events. Greek-theatre seasons run in summer, opera houses generally begin their seasons in the autumn, while concert series are held at the beaches all summer long. Folk festivals, religious festivals celebrating holy days or the feast days of patron saints (every town has at least one) and sagre (food festivals) take place throughout the year. Check with the local tourist office to see what is on during your stay (and see pp26–7).

For special events and details on performances, check with local tourist offices or consult the fortnightly pamphlet *Lapis*. This is the definitive resource for music, plays, drama, puppet theatre, readings, cinema, dance and art exhibitions, with complete listings of venues. It is distributed free in Palermo and Catania versions, each covering one half of the island (*www.lapispalermo.it for Palermo or www.lapisnet.it for Catania*).

CINEMA

Complete listings are available in *Lapis*. Italians prefer dubbing to subtitles but under the Learn By Movies programme, the University of Catania offers free screenings of films in their original language at the Cinema Odeon (*Via Filippo Corridoni 19, Catania. Tel: (095) 326 324. Mondays at 8.30 & 10.30pm*).

NIGHTLIFE

Nightlife in Sicily does not necesssarily conjure up the same images as it might in other cultures. Although the two main cities are lively at night, in smaller towns most people opt for a *passeggiata* (evening stroll). During summer, small towns are quite successful at organising festivals, at the very least providing live music in a central piazza. There is a wealth of opportunity to hear live world music in various venues from public gardens to clubs to small theatres.

Nightclubs and discos can be found in the two main cities and in beach resorts, where seaside lidos are transformed into casual *discoteche* by night. There is not a drinking culture as such, and abuse of alcohol is extremely rare.

Catania

The heart of Catania's famed nightlife is centred on the area around the Scalinata Alessi, or staircase, heading up from Via Alessi to Via Crociferi not far from Piazza dell'Università. Here there is an endless array of clubs and bars.

Palermo

Piazza all'Olivella, full of festive crowds until the wee hours, is a good starting point for club hopping in the area. Accross Via Maqueda, head to Via dei Candelai, location of the eponymous bar among others.

At Kursaal Kalhesa, cavernous spaces carved from the interior of the city's walls combine a wine bar, bookshop and restaurant for a pleasant, but non-raucous atmosphere; there are concert series here in summer. For more of a party scene, try the same management's magical Kursaal Tonnara, on the western edge of the city in an ancient *tonnara* (tuna fishery); a restaurant and hotel are also located here.

Kursaal Kalhesa, Foro Umberto I 21. Tel: (091) 616 2111.
www.kursaalkalhesa.it
Kursaal Tonnara, Vergine Maria,
Via Bordonaro 9. Tel: (091) 637 2267.
www.kursaaltonnara.it

MUSIC, THEATRE AND THE ARTS

Agrigento

Classical music is performed during July within the Valle dei Templi in the lush Kolymbetra Gardens.

Valle dei Templi, Agritenti, Giardino della Kolymbetra. Tel: (335) 122 9042.

Catania

Teatro Massimo Bellini

Since 1890, Catania's neoclassical theatre has been offering a full season of symphonic music and opera plus off-season performances.

Perrotta 12. Tel: (095) 730 6111.
www.teatromassimobellini.it

Zō

In Catania's old sulphur works, this centre for contemporary culture is a

Entertainment

Teatro Massimo in Palermo

'factory for cultural events'. The enormous and varied structure contains spaces for exhibitions, performance art and music. There is a café and restaurant on site.
Piazzale Asia 6. Tel: (095) 533 871. www.zoculture.it

Erice
Music Festival
During the months of July and August, in the Castello di Venere and in historic churches throughout the medieval centre, the Accademia Musicale di Palermo organises performances of jazz, classical and medieval music.
Tel: (091) 323 887. www.comune.erice.tp.it

Palermo
Festival sul Novecento Palermo
Palermo's October celebration of the 20th century offers guided tours of the city's newly restored monuments, theatres and churches. There is also an extensive programme of events that includes contemporary music, drama, film and dance.
Information available from Palermo Tourist Information Office (see p38).

Kals'Art
In La Kalsa district, gallery shows, live music, film and theatre performances presented in the piazzas and venues of the old Arab quarter, during July and August.
Information available from Palermo Tourist Information Office (see p38).

Politeama Garibaldi
Founded in the early 1900s as a theatre for the people, the Politeama offers a traditional season of symphonic music from November to June.
Piazza Ruggero Settimo. Tel: (091) 322 777. www.orchestrasinfonicasiciliana.it

Lo Spasimo
In La Kalsa district, the now-roofless 16th-century church of Santa Maria dello Spasimo and its gardens provide an enchanting venue for films, art exhibitions and concerts.
Piazza Spasimo. Tel: (091) 616 1486.

Teatro Biondo Stabile
Concerts, modern theatre, dramatic readings and events, some free of charge, at Palermo's 19th-century theatre, built with the middle class in mind.
Via Roma 258. Tel: (091) 743 431. www.teatrobiondo.it

Teatro Massimo
Since 1897, the year-long season offers performances of opera, symphonic music and classical dance.
Piazza Giuseppe Verdi. Tel: (091) 605 3521.

Ancient theatres
The consortium of ancient venues in Sicily, Teatri di Pietra, organises performances and publishes information in one central spot.

The Greek Theatre in Siracusa stages classical drama in May and June

Among others, it represents the Greek theatres of Morgantina, Eraclea Minoa, Palazzolo Acreide and ancient venues such as the Temple of Hera at Selinunte.
www.teatridipietra.org (Italian only)

Segesta Teatro Greco

With a breathtaking view all the way to the Golfo di Castellammare as the backdrop, modern theatre, classical drama, dance and concerts are staged during the summer season.
Tel: (0924) 953 013.
www.festivalsegesta.com. Box office on site opens 2 hrs before a performance.

Siracusa Teatro Greco

The home of the Istituto Nazionale del Dramma Antico presents classical drama in a season that usually covers May and June in Siracusa and travels throughout Sicily and the world in July and August.
Corso Matteotti 29, Siracusa. Tel: (0931) 487 200. www.indafondazione.org

Taormina Teatro Greco

From July to September, concerts, theatre and dance are performed in Taormina's famed Greek Theatre.
Palazzo dei Congressi, Piazza Vittorio Emanuele 7, Taormina. Tel: (0942) 626 124. www.taormina-arte.com

Tindari Teatro Greco

With the Tyrrhenian Sea as scenery, classical and modern drama as well as concerts are staged during August at ancient Tindari's Greek theatre.
Near Patti on the north coast.
Tel: (091) 626 0177.

Food and drink

Food is one of the pleasures of visiting Sicily and an integral facet of the island's history and culture. From the simplest to the most sophisticated, dishes are made to traditional recipes using fresh, often locally grown ingredients.

See the features on Desserts and pastries (pp164–5), Sicilian wines (pp166–7) and on olive oil (pp150–51).

SICILIAN CUISINE

Sicily's cuisine is clearly marked as Mediterranean – it's based on fresh seasonal produce, olive oil, wine and wheat – but just as modern Sicily is a palimpsest of the cultures that dominated the island in centuries past, so is the cuisine.

In the ancient eras, chefs used fresh fish and vinegar, a combination still used in Siracusa. Olives and grapes were cultivated by the Greeks, if they had not been grown before then. The Arabs brought in sugar cane, pistachio, sesame, citrus fruits, jasmine, rice, cinnamon, saffron and, importantly, the formula for making dried pasta. Novelties from the New World were introduced by the Spanish: potatoes, chocolate, prickly-pear cactus, peppers and tomatoes.

The modern face of Sicilian cuisine evolved from both the *cucina povera* – poor-man's food that takes advantage of the wide varieties of grains and vegetables – and the repertoire of the

monsù. The kitchens of the noble class had French influences from the 1300s, reinforced in the 1800s and 1900s by French-trained chefs known as *monsù*, a Sicilian corruption of *monsieur*. Traces of their recipes are still seen in, for example, *timballi*, *gallantine* and the nearly ubiquitous fish, meat or vegetable *involtini* (roulades).

A rich selection of *materia prima* (ingredients) cultivated in Sicily's ideal conditions gives personality to the cuisine: capers, sea salt, oregano, olives, olive oil, honey, almonds, pistachio, the impossibily long *cucuzza* squash with its furry leaves called *tenerrumi*, artichokes, superb hard wheat that makes almost spicy tasting breads and pastas, all manner of citrus, the freshest of fresh fish and the list goes on.

Regional specialties

Particularly Sicilian are *caponata* (sweet and sour aubergine); orange, fennel and olive salad; ricotta in all its many forms; marinated fresh

A butcher in Poggioreale displays his sausages

anchovies; *sarde a beccafico* (baked sardines stuffed with breadcrumbs and citrus fruit); and *involtini* (meat rolls). Notice as the landscape changes from region to region, so do the shapes of the breads, the methods of preparing fish, the cheeses and pastries. There is a common thread but each region presents its own particular versions.

In **Palermo** province you'll find *pasta con le sarde* (with fresh sardines and wild fennel fronds) and *sfincione* (an oniony pizza). In Palermo and the northwest, you can make a light lunch of *pane consatu*, a sandwich minimally dressed with olive oil and flavourings such as anchovy or cheese, with tomato or onion rubbed into the bread.

In the **northwest**, as witness to the island's proximity to North Africa, you'll find couscous on menus, savoury with fish or sweet with honey. Tuna run off the northwest coast, hence fresh tuna is eaten in spring, and a good selection of preserved tuna can be found. In Trapani, hollow, spaghetti-like pasta called *busiatti* are served with *pesto alla Trapanese* (tomatoes, garlic and almonds pestled with a little basil).

In the mountainous interior of the **central** part of the island, taste aromatic sausages, pork terrines, grilled lamb and hearty pasta sauces. A wide range of cheeses is made from both sheep's milk as well as goat's milk from the Capra Girgentana breed.

In the **northeast**, swordfish has long had a place in the kitchen; it can be grilled, stuffed, rolled or paired with mint on pasta. Look for *mostarda*, grape must reduced to chewy candy-like consistency, pistachio pastries made from nuts cultivated in groves at Bronte on Etna, and the national dish of Catania – Pasta alla Norma – which has a sauce of barely cooked tomatoes with garlic and basil, topped with strips of fried aubergine and a generous sprinkling of *ricotta salata* (ricotta salted and aged until of grating consistency).

In the **southeast**, there is a concentration of creative chefs who are keeping tradition alive not by faithfully reproducing old recipes but by intelligently enriching their inherited patrimony so as to carry it a step into the future. Traditional dishes include tuna, bread pockets called *schiacce* stuffed simply with ricotta and sausage or parsley and onion, sweet and sour rabbit *alla stemperata*, and elaborate pastries (*see pp164–5*).

MEALS

Listed on a menu as *antipasti* (starters), expect to find small, creative versions of streetfood such as *arancini* (rice balls coated with breadcrumbs) and *panelle* (chickpea fritters) or small plates of fresh fish or vegetables. Pastas under the *primi* (first courses) section of the menu are offered with a huge variety of sauces, giving you an opportunity to sample some vegetables and also taste some traditional or contemporary combinations. *Secondi* (main dishes) may be elaborately prepared recipes but are more often simply roasted or grilled fresh fish or meat. Salads and vegetables are listed under *contorni* and take full advantage of the flavours of the island: you may see a salad of cherry tomatoes, capers and anchovies; sweet and sour caponata; sautéed greens, and many others. Artisanal cheeses, fresh fruit or *dolci* (desserts) are offered as a close to the meal. While the order of the courses is to be respected, there is no need to order one of each; feel free to mix and match as you like. Vegetarians rejoice as there are myriad options for varied meals based solely on vegetable ingredients.

Mealtimes

Restaurants usually open from 12.30 until 2.30pm for lunch and from 8pm until midnight for dinner. It is

Cannoli di ricotta taste as delicious as they look

presumed that you will linger at your table for as long as you wish, so when you're ready to leave you must ask for the *conto* (bill). A small tip of a few euro is much appreciated by waiting staff, but not an obligation.

DRINKS

As in the rest of Italy, superb coffee is served in a number of different ways, although this far south you might find it is very strong. If you'd prefer a big cup of less strong coffee ask for a *caffè americano*.

Restaurants and bars usually offer bottled water, either *frizzante* (sparkling) or *naturale* (flat).

International-brand soft drinks are available but why not opt for a more local drink – try tangy *gassosa* (citrus soda), slightly bitter yet thirst-quenching *chinotto* (quinine soda) or a refreshing *latte di mandorla* (almond milk).

Sicilian wines (*see pp166–7*) are remarkably evocative: you can taste the flavours of the island's breeze, sun and earth in a glass. Exchange ideas with the sommeliers to let them know what you're most interested in. If wine pairings are offered with a menu, that's a good way to get to know several different wines in the context for which they were created. After dinner, sip *un marsala*. The oxidative perfumes of the island's historic fortified wine are like the overlapping layers of the island's grand history.

Food and drink

WHERE TO EAT

Prices vary widely and these should only be used as a rough guide.

The following prices are per person, for a three-course meal excluding wine.

★ Under 30 euros
★★ 30–35 euros
★★★ 35–45 euros
★★★★ Over 45 euros

Please note that Addiopizzo is an anti-Mafia organisation where business owners have bravely clubbed together to stand up to Mafia demands for protection money.

Palermo

Antica Focacceria San Francesco ★
Founded in 1834, this is a good venue to try the epitome of Palermitan street food, *pan ca meusa* (spleen sandwich), or go for a pasta or a salad instead. Classic 19th-century décor; outdoor seating in the charming piazza at the front.
Via A Paternostro 58. Tel: (091) 320 624. Member Addiopizzo.

Piccolo Napoli ★★
A family operation with an old-fashioned dining room and superb, simple fresh fish.
Piazzetta Mulino a Vento 4. Tel: (091) 320 431.

Sant'Andrea ★★
In a small piazza in the Vucciria, the romantic setting and well-prepared dishes make this a perennial choice for a good meal.
Piazzetta Sant'Andrea 4. Tel: (091) 334 999. Open: Mon–Sat.

Dispensa dei Monsù ★★★
Lovely small restaurant where the chef-owner prepares recipes from her family's repertoire using the best of ingredients. Excellent selection of wines. Dinner only. Reservations necessary.
Via Principe di Villafranca 59. Tel: (091) 609 0465. Member Addiopizzo.

Marzipan fruit is a Sicilian favourite

Kursaal Khalesa ★★★
One of the most interesting venues in Palermo with restrained modern preparations of traditional foods, this bar/bookshop/restaurant is located by the sea inside the old city walls (*see p153*).
Foro Umberto I 21.
Tel: (091) 616 2282.
Member Addiopizzo.

Northwest Sicily
La Pineta ★
Casual beachside restaurant serving extremely fresh fish; tables set on the sand or 'inside'.
Via Punta Cantone, Marinella di Selinunte.
Tel: (0924) 46 820.

Al Porticciolo Ristorante e Pizzeria ★★
This casual restaurant near Cefalù's small port is always recommended by locals. Fresh fish is on display, there's a great view of the water, and their pizzeria two doors down makes good use of its wood-burning oven.
Via Carlo Ortolani di Bordonaro 86–90, Cefalù.
Tel: (0921) 423 151.
Open: daily in summer, Tue–Sun in winter.

Da Gioacchino ★★
Family run, family style. Pizza and good, simple mountain foods: sausages, grilled lamb, excellent cheeses.
Via Garibaldi 1, Poggioreale.
Tel: (0924) 75 925.

Le Lumie ★★
A modern building with terrace and dining room by Lo Stagnone with views of the Egadi Islands and romantic sunsets. The young chef is devoted to his craft and makes the most of the ingredients from the territory; great wine list.
Contrada Fontanelle 178 B, Marsala.
Tel: (0923) 995 197.
Open: Thur–Tue.

Le Mura ★★
Fresh seafood caught locally is served by the sea in the airy and pleasant historic centre of Trapani.
Viale delle Sirene 15, Trapani.
Tel: (0923) 872 622.

Monte San Giuliano ★★
Excellent couscous with flecks of almonds mixed into the *semola* served on a quaint terrace in the medieval centre of Erice.

Vicolo S Rocco, Erice.
Tel: (0923) 869 595.

Il Bavaglino ★★★
A miniscule, Art Deco interior expands on to a terrace for outdoor dining in summer. Creative dishes based on family recipes lovingly prepared by young chef Giuseppe Costa.
Via Benedetto Saputo 20, Terrasini. Tel: (091) 868 2285. Open: Wed–Mon.

Northeast Sicily
Bottega dell'Etna ★
A old-fashioned dry-goods shop with a few Sicilian specialities served at two plastic tables or wrapped for taking away (or up – this is a great place to stop for provisions if you're heading up Mount Etna).
Via Umberto 89, Linguaglossa.
Tel: (095) 643 544.

Osteria Nero d'Avola ★★
The charismatic *oste* (host) Turi Siligato is an ambassador for small producers and a master of hospitality. He works with the best of the region's artisanal producers and offers easy-going tasting menus

in a cosy courtyard in Taormina.

Vico De Spuches 8, Taormina. Tel: (0942) 628 874.

Shalai ★★

Comfortably elegant interior, Sicilian and international recipes delicately and expertly prepared. Small, carefully selected wine list.

Via Guglielmo Marconi 25, Linguaglossa. Tel: (095) 643 128.

Tischi Toschi ★★

Abundant dishes of excellently prepared, flavourful home cooking, Messina style. Let Luca the chef fill your table with savoury treats.

Via Mario Aspa 9, Messina.
Tel: (090) 51 745.

La Capinera ★★★

Highly regarded for the professionalism of chef Pietro d'Agostino, creative fresh fish, fair prices and a beautiful setting on the sea just below Taormina.

Via Nazionale 177, Spisone, Taormina Mare. Tel: (0942) 626 247. Open: Tue–Sun.

Central Sicily

La Ferla ★

Casual trattoria with a kitchen that turns out abundant platters of deeply satisfying local preparations: hearty vegetable pastas, grilled lamb, roasted artichokes and local cheeses.

Via Roma 29, Caltabellota. Tel: (0925) 951 444. Open: Nov–Sept Tue–Sun.

Agriturismo Mandranova ★★

Mother and son team up in the kitchen of this pristine *agriturismo*. Sip an *aperitivo* in the garden and enjoy the clean flavours of their well-prepared food on the candlelit terrace. Reservations necessary.

Contrada Mandranova, SS 115 km 271, Palma di Montechiaro.
Tel: (393) 986 21 69.

Trattoria dei Templi ★★

This family-run trattoria is a very good option and is near the archaeological park.

Via Panoramica dei Templi 15, Agrigento. Tel: (0922) 403 110. Open: summer Mon–Sat, rest of year Sat–Thur.

Trattoria la Vecchia Conza ★★

Portside in Sciacca, feast on a never-ending array of fresh fish. It's always packed with locals, so book ahead.

Via Pietro Gerardi 39, Sciacca. Tel: (0925) 25 385. Open: Tue–Sun.

Ristorante Coria ★★★

Inspired by Sicilian gastronomic historian Giuseppe Coria, author of *Profumi di Sicilia*, the classic compilation of Sicilian recipes, the entire island is represented in both kitchen and cellar.

Via Infermeria 24, Caltagirone. Tel: (0933) 334 615. Open: Tue–Sun lunchtime.

La Madia ★★★★

The thoughtful creations of chef Pino Cuttaia are designed to pique all the senses harmoniously; delicately balanced dishes with deep flavours.

Corso F Re Capriata 22, Licata. Tel: (0922) 771 443. Open: Mon–Sat.

Southeast Sicily

Ristorante Crocifisso di Marco Baglieri ★

Down-home Neatino cooking from Marco

Baglieri who stays mostly in the kitchen, yelling out menu suggestions to his regulars. Great plates of mixed antipasti include fried ricotta and hearty pastas, plus traditional main courses with local wines to match.
Via Principe Umberto 48, Noto (Alta). Tel: (0931) 571 151. Open: Thur–Tue.

Ristorante Pomara ★
Meat barbecued over the open stone fireplace is the speciality of the house.
Via Vittorio Veneto 84, San Michele di Ganzaria. Tel: (0933) 978 032.

Sapori Perduti ★
Old-fashioned recipes from Modica's rich gastronomic tradition. Comfortable interior and outdoor seating available right on the lively corso. There's a good chance a musician will blow a few harmonica tunes from a nearby doorway.
Corso Umberto I 228, Modica. Tel: (0932) 944 247.

Albergo Ristorante Antica Filanda ★★
The high-quality yet reasonably priced food, the great wine list and the views merit a

pilgrimage to the Nebrodi Mountains.
Strada Provinciale 157, Capri Leone. Tel: (0941) 919 704.

La Cialoma ★★
A *cialoma* is the work song sung by tuna fishermen, and here in the most romantic piazza, not just in Sicily but in all of Italy, La Cialoma serves simply and excellently prepared fresh fish. Great atmosphere, cheery service and possibly the best tuna on the island.
Piazza Regina Margherita 23, Marzamemi. Tel: (0931) 841 772. Open: summer daily, rest of year Wed–Mon.

Locandina ★★
This is a good, informal option in Ragusa Ibla. Gorgeous interior, innovative dishes, pizza and interesting wines.
Via Orfanotrofio 39, Ragusa Ibla. Tel: (0932) 220 031.

Trattoria La Foglia ★★★
The menu covers the basics and includes the excellent, hearty, home-style greens the Mediterranean diet is based upon. In the heart

of Siracusa *centro*, it's like eating in your grandmother's house, if she were a slightly batty, down-at-the-heels Sicilian noblewoman.
Via Capodiece 29, Siracusa.
Tel: (0931) 66 233.

La Gazza Ladra ★★★★
Chef Accursio Craparo is one of the truly creative souls working in the southeast of Sicily. He translates his sensations of his home territory into beautifully crafted dishes with layers of flavour. Sommelier Mauro Mattei is prepared and professional.
Hotel Palazzo Failla, Via Blandini 11, Modica (Alta). Tel: (0932) 755 655. Open: Tue–Sun lunchtime.

Ristorante Duomo ★★★★
In this supremely elegant restaurant, expert waiters anticipate your every desire at lunch and dinner. Chef Ciccio Sultano expresses his bubbly personality in his food.
Via Capitano Bocchierie 31, Ragusa Ibla.
Tel: (0932) 651 265.
Open: daily for dinner, Tue–Sat lunchtime.

Desserts and pastries

Most of the basic ingredients and some of the fundamental recipes of Sicily's world-famous sweets are thanks to the Arabs, while chocolate was imported straight from Mexico into Modica. Chocolatiers there still process it cold, leaving sugar crystals intact.

For centuries, nuns in Sicilian convents earned their keep selling sweets made from ingredients grown on their lands. Only a few still practise this tradition but some local pastry-makers have managed to get hold of monastic recipes so their secrets have not been lost to the grave.

Sicilian *cassata*

Cannolo di ricotta

The apotheosis of Sicilian sweets, a pastry tube is shaped around a piece of *canna* (reed), fried and filled with creamy, sweetened ricotta sometimes with added candied fruit, lemon zest or bits of chocolate.

Cassata

This cake, a gift of Arab dominion refined by the Spanish, is supremely light when made well. *Pan di Spagna* (sponge cake) supports a sweet ricotta filling all of which is covered by sheets of pistachio and almond marzipan, elaborately garnished with white icing and candied fruits.

Gelo

Delicately perfumed jellies were brought in under Arabic rule and enriched by the *monsù* (*see p156*). Pink watermelon *gelo* is garnished with jasmine flowers and pistachios; other versions are made of lemon, carob flour or almond milk when it becomes *biancomangiare* (blancmange).

Granita

The Romans flavoured the snows of Mount Etna as a summer refresher. Today these slushes are flavoured with fruit, coffee or almond milk.

Gelato

Gelato was discovered in the mid-1500s, although by whom remains a mystery. It was, though, a Sicilian who made the alluring creaminess of the delicately balanced emulsion of sugar, water, fat and air available to the masses. Francesco Procopio Cutò, a fisherman born in Catania province, perfected a gelato machine designed by his grandfather and put it into action in 1686 when he opened Le Procope, one of the first coffee houses in Paris.

A typical display in a pasticceria

Dolci modicani

In the area around Modica and Noto, don't miss 'mpanatighi, a sweet empanada stuffed with chocolate and ground beef; cubbaita or giuggiulena, a honey and sesame torrone (nougat); nucatuli, with dried figs inside a pastry crust; and delicately spiced carruba or carob jellies and biscuits.

Frutta della Martorana

The sisters of the Palermitan convent, commonly called the Martorana, invented these sweets on the occasion of a wintertime visit from their bishop: the fruit trees of their courtyard were bare so they created little marzipan fruits to hang from the branches and impress their visitor. The best versions are freakishly realistic, while the confections turned out as cheap souvenirs are luridly coloured and a touch too shiny.

Pastry shops

Pasticceria Maria Grammatico, Via Vittorio Emanuele 14, Erice. Tel: (0923) 869 390.

Pasticceria Irrera, Piazza Cairoli, Messina. Tel: (090) 641 3640.

Antica Dolceria Bonajuto, Corso Umberto I 159, Modica. Tel: (0932) 941 225.

Donna Elvira, Via Risorgimento 32, Modica. Tel: (0932) 764 359.

Caffé Sicilia, Corso Vittorio Emanuele III 125, Noto. Tel: (0931) 835 013.

Bam Bar Granite, Via di Giovanni 45, Taormina. Tel: (0942) 24 355.

Pasticceria Colicchia, Via delle Arti 6, Trapani. Tel: (0923) 547 612.

Abbeys

Abbazia di Santo Spirito, Via Santo Spirito 8, Agrigento.

Abbazia di San Michele, Piazza San Michele, Mazara del Vallo.

Sicilian wines

History

Romantically, it was a tear shed by Dionysius that germinated the first grape vine in Sicily. Palaeontology, however, dates grape growing on the island to the 15th century BC. During the ancient eras, Sicilian wine was lauded for its quality and produced in quantities for trade and export. In the 20th century, while more northerly European wine-producing zones gained fame, Sicily remained behind the scenes. From ports around the island, wines grown in Sicily's ideal conditions were shipped north, incognito, to enhance the body and flavour of wines born in less fortunate climes.

Beginning with the Tasca d'Almerita family's efforts at their estate Regaleali in the 1960s, Sicilian growers began coaxing high-quality wines from their vineyards, bottling them and marketing them proudly as Sicilian. Their headway was furthered by the efforts of the Planeta family whose successes in winemaking and marketing have not only confirmed the presence of Sicilian wines on the world market but on a broader scale have helped spread awareness of Sicilian culture.

Grillo grapes growing in the sandy soil near Marsala

Attention first brought to Sicilian wine production with help from the so-called international varieties, but now, with a more knowledgeable and sophisticated base of consumers, producers are focusing on the expression of *terroir* best achieved with autochthonous varieties.

Marsala wine bottles

Growing areas

Nero d'Avola may be the most well-known Sicilian grape, and while it has naturalised around the island, it is actually from Avola in the southeast. Its more elegant cousin, Frappato, is also indigenous to the southeast, particularly to the zone of Vittoria in the Ragusano. When Frappato is blended with Nero d'Avola, the result is the spicy, elegant Cersuolo di Vittoria. Among a host of valid productions, look for bottles from the farms of Arianna Occhipinti, COS or Gulfi.

The traditional reds grown in Mount Etna's black soils are Nerello Mascalese and Nerello Capuccio; the main white from the mountain is Carricante. A few minor cultivars, both white and, as they say, black, manage to survive, held from the brink of extinction by a few sensitive farmers who appreciate the balance they bring to blends with the main grapes. Bottles to keep an eye out for bear the names of Benanti, Biondi, Frank Cornelissen, Graci, I Vigneri and Tenute delle Terre Nere.

The reds of Punto Faro, north of the city of Messina, are created from the same varieties grown on Etna together with a red particular to the point, Nocera. The cool conditions and dramatically different geology produce fresh, yet profound wines. Few producers work this tiny denomination. Look for Palari and Bonavita; the latter also tempts palates with a bottling of an enticing *rosato*.

In the west of Sicily, the red Perriconem, or Pignatello, is being brought back from the brink of extinction. White varietals like Inzolia, Cattarato, Grillo and Zibbibo (this one vinified dry and also sweet – as for Passito di Pantelleria) manage to stand up to the brutal heat, dry conditions and occasional buffeting by the sirocco that whips up from the Sahara. Among the many valid producers, search for Barraco, Guccione, Ferrandes, Porta del Vento and Marco de Bartoli.

Children

Travelling with children in Sicily should present no problems, as there are reasonable facilities in terms of healthcare, travel, eating and accommodation, and good hygiene. There is also much to interest and entertain children, especially older ones, in terms of historical interest and sights. Sicilians love children, so they may be made a big fuss of, especially if they have fair hair and blue eyes.

Children's health

Public toilets are not very common in Sicily, but may be found in parks, by the beach or near the *comune* (government building). There should be no problem about using toilets in bars and cafés, as long as you are buying at least a coffee or water in return. Some spare toilet paper or tissues might be useful.

Remember to use sunblock as often as possible. Anti-bacterial hand-wash gel or hand-wipes are effective ways of ensuring good hygiene when travelling.

If travelling with a baby, *farmacie* (pharmacies) sell baby formula as well as sterilising solutions. Disposable nappies are cheapest at supermarkets. In some remote villages, only UHT milk is available.

Sicily's food is well suited to children's tastes, with a wide range of pasta, pizza, rice and snacks available. *Granita*, a summer drink made with crushed ice and fresh fruit juice, is a firm favourite, not to mention the superb range of ice creams on offer.

Family fun

It is worth asking at tourist offices as to whether there are attractions or events geared to families. After all, you can get saturated with art galleries and archaeological museums! It is also worth researching hotels in advance, to ensure that they cater for children.

A favourite with kids is the traditional Sicilian puppet theatre, with shows in Palermo, at the **Museo Internazionale delle Marionette**, and in Cefalù, at the **Opera dei Pupi**. In fact, both Palermo and Cefalù are good children's destinations, as both have beaches. Palermo's nearest one is at Mondello, a popular resort especially in the summer. Another great town for kids is Taormina, with superb views, cultural attractions, beaches nearby, and an exciting cable-car trip to take you down to the coast.

If video games are your children's thing, then **Goethe Games** in Palermo may be an enjoyable escape for them. There are video games to suit all tastes as well as billiards and a 'video music' section.

Museo Internazionale delle Marionette, Piazzetta Niscemi 1, Palermo. Tel: (091) 328 060.

Opera dei Pupi, Corso Ruggero, Cefalù. Tel: (092) 192 4188.

Goethe Games, Via Goethe 63, Palermo. Tel: (091) 611 8149.

Out and about

A trip to a volcano makes for an exciting day out for children. One option is to take the cable car up Mount Etna, and see the volcano from close up. After dark, the incandescent eruptions and lava flows are a magical sight. The Aeolian Islands offer volcano experiences on a much smaller scale, with the added attraction of boat tours to secluded sandy beaches, where one can jump from the boat into crystalline waters. Remember to pack swimming goggles so you can explore underwater life, especially volcanic gases bubbling up from the bottom of the sea!

See the chapter on Getting Away From It All (*pp140–45*) for details of beaches and other suitable activities for kids.

Useful tips

Some handy tips for travelling families:

- Try to teach children a few words of Italian so that they can have fun ordering in restaurants.
- Children love to record their memories: a simple camera, scrapbook and glue for sticking in tickets, photos, postcards, etc, will allow them to keep a holiday book of their experiences.
- Pick a hotel with a pool or a nearby beach so that kids can have a break from sightseeing.
- Have a siesta during the hottest part of the day to avoid the risk of heat exhaustion and dehydration.
- Let children have a say in the daily itinerary and, if they are old enough, let them research and guide the family on a day's outing.
- Try to mix with the locals at events like village festivals to enjoy the experience to the full.
- Dark churches can be fun for children, especially if they are allowed to put change in the donation box, work the coin-operated illuminations or light candles.

Children will love trying out the watersports

Sport and leisure

Sicilians love summer and spending their days on the beach, so watersports are popular – everything from scuba diving to jet skiing and snorkelling to sailing. Traditional family life tends to rank more highly in importance than the ideal of 'work hard, play hard' that exists in other countries, however, so families tend to undertake sports together. As in many other countries, football draws in the biggest crowds.

Golf

Sicily has four 18-hole golf courses. One is within easy driving distance of Catania – quite a challenging course, set in a superb location with Mount Etna in the background.
Picciolo Golf Club. Castiglione di Licilio, Linguaglossa. Tel: (0920) 298 6252.

Le Madonie is set on the north coast, overlooking the sea, a 15-minute drive from Cefalù. *Cosoda Bartuccelli, Collesano. Tel: (0921) 934 387. www.lemadoniegolf.com*

Two 18-hole courses and one 9-hole course and driving range are part of the Verdura resort in the southwest at Sciacca.
Verdura Golf and Spa Resort, Contrada Verdura, Sciacca. Tel: (0925) 99 8001.

A helpful site for golf enthusiasts is *www.sicilygolf.com*

Skiing and horse riding

Facilities for both are available in Etna Madonie and Nebrodi nature reserves (*see pp143–4*).

Watersports

Many visitors to Sicily spend much of their time in or near the water, which is understandable considering the superb clarity of the sea and the range of places where you can enjoy it.

Scuba diving and snorkelling

The most popular dive and snorkelling sites are in the Aeolian Islands. The biggest island, Lipari, has several dive centres, from where you can venture to different dive sites around the islands, such as Stromboli. Dive conditions are at their best between May and October. Other notable dive sites are:

Isola Bella, near Taormina. The waters here are calm and therefore ideal for beginners. Dropping down to 12m (39ft), this location is good for try dives.

Scopello, on the Bay of Castellammare in northwest Sicily. Some of the dive sites are a boat ride from the shore, such as the Impisu Wall, which drops to 135m (443ft) deep, and Ficarella Cave. There are

World War II wrecks to be seen, and fishes including Mediterranean groupers and damselfish.

Ustica Island, 60km (37^1/$_2$ miles) north of Palermo. This small island has some of the clearest waters and best-preserved marine reserves anywhere in the Mediterranean, helped by its isolation. The best dive sites are Scoglio del Medico (Doctor's Rock) and Secca Colombara.

The **Egadi Islands**. Dive companies in Marsala can take you the 15 minutes by boat to the beautiful Egadi Islands.

Windsurfing and sailing

Most of Sicily's seaside resorts are suitable for windsurfing, although the places generally regarded as best are the Aeolian Islands and the Capo Passero area, at the southeastern tip of the island where the Ionian and Mediterranean seas converge.

Sailing is popular too in Sicily, especially along the northern coast, with yachts from all over Europe sailing around Sicilian waters. Nautical tourism is growing fast, and as a result, sailing facilities have improved dramatically over the past few years. Boats can be chartered or rented from nautical clubs and organisations on most of the islands off Sicily, including the Aeolian Islands, Ustica, Pantelleria and the Pelagie Islands.

Sport and leisure

A surfer on Cefalù beach

Accommodation

Accommodation in Sicily has greatly improved of late, reflecting the relatively new-found interest in travelling to points beyond the two cities and traditional resort areas. Catering for tourists is still not as advanced as on the coast and in the cities, and the hoteliers in the east are more in tune with modern tastes and expectations for services than those in the west, although the gap is closing.

WHERE TO STAY

The hotels listed below are mostly full-service hotels with a few offering the option of self-catering.

Prices

August is considered 'highest' season and prices reflect it. The prices below are for a double room in spring or autumn.

★	Under 100 euros
★★	100–150 euros
★★★	150–200 euros
★★★★	More than 200 euros

Palermo
SoleLuna B&B della Solidarietà ★

In an apartment building in the newer section of Palermo, each bedroom is colourfully decorated and has its own private, though not en-suite, bathroom. Five per cent of proceeds are donated to a local youth group.
Via Vincenzo Riolo 7.
Tel: (091) 581 671.
www.solelunabedandbreakfast.org

BB22 ★★

Charming small hotel in the Vucciria. Playful, modern décor mixes well with the lines of the old palace. Great location and a reasonable price for a very comfortable hotel.
Largo Cavalieri di Malta 22.
Tel: (091) 611 1610.
www.bb22.it

Centrale Palace ★★

Steps from Quattro Canti, an 18th-century palace restored into an elegant hotel with garage, gym and roof terrace for meals.
Corso Vittorio Emanuele 327.
Tel: (091) 336 666.
www.angalahotels.it

Kursaal Tonnara ★★★

An ancient tuna fishery on the edge of the city has been transformed into a restaurant, bar, event space and boutique hotel with enormous, stylish rooms.
Via Bordonaro 9.
Tel: (091) 637 2267.
www.kursaaltonnara.it

Northwest Sicily

Ai Lumi ★

In a Baroque palazzo on Trapani's pedestrian corso, this small hotel offers both B&B and self-catering apartments. Restaurant and wine bar in the same building.
Corso Vittorio Emanuele 75, Trapani. Tel: (0923) 540 922. www.ailumi.it

Pensione Tranchina ★

Casual, central small hotel with very nice staff and small restaurant (half-board option available). Most of the clean, perfectly serviceable rooms have terraces with views over the village or sea.
Via A Diaz 7, Scopello. Tel: (0924) 541 099. www. pensionetranchina.com

Planeta Estate la Foresteria ★★

Large comfortable rooms in this chic new hotel have views out over the Planeta vineyards to the sea, plus pool, wine and oil tastings, and cookery lessons. A good base for exploring from Selinunte to Agrigento and the Belice Valley.
Contrada Passo di Gurra ex, SS 115 km 91, Menfi.

Tel: (0925) 195 5460. www.planetaestate.it

La Plumeria ★★

This hotel in a renovated palazzo in Cefalù's historic centre opened in August 2010: very comfortable rooms, parquet throughout, engaging staff and free parking.
Corso Ruggero 185, Cefalù.
Tel: (0921) 925 897. www.laplumeriahotel.it

Relais Antiche Saline ★★

Spacious, clean, rather spare rooms with views over the Egadi Islands and the salt pans of Trapani's coast. Lovely courtyard and pool area; restaurant on site. Near Trapani's airport.
Via Verdi, località Nubia, Paceco.
Tel: (0923) 868 029. www. hotelantichesaline.com

Tenuta Gangivecchio ★★

In the heart of the Madonie Mountains, an inn, cottage, restaurant and cookery school are housed in a 14th-century abbey with lush grounds. The owners provide detailed suggestions for hiking and touring in the area.

5km (3 miles) from Gangi.
Tel: (0921) 644 804. www.gangivecchio.org

Tonnara di Scopello ★★

Self-catering apartments within what is perhaps the most gorgeous scenery on the entire island and a rare chance to stay in a historic tuna fishery, making up for uneven service and the quirks of an ancient building.
Tonnara di Scopello.
Tel: (339) 307 1970. www. tonnaradiscopello.com

Northeast Sicily

Hotel Villa Schuler ★★

Comfortable, low-key option for Taormina. Rooms have views of the sea or the hotel gardens; breakfast is served on the terrace overlooking the Gulf of Naxos.
Via Roma, Piazzetta Bastione, Taormina.
Tel: (0942) 23 481. www.hotelvillaschuler.com

Hotel Signum ★★★

Romantic island get-away on the slopes of Salina. Spa, pool, private bungalows and excellent restaurant.

Via Scalo 15, Malfa, Salina. Tel: (090) 984 4222. www.hotelsignum.it

Katane Palace ★★★

This modern hotel is a good option in Catania centre with attentive staff. Garage parking on request.

Via Finocchiaro Aprile 110, Catania.
Tel: (095) 747 0702.
www.katanepalace.it

Piccolo Giardino ★★★

Light-filled rooms in this new hotel in Taormina's historic centre and a great view of Castelmola from the pool. Parking can be arranged.

Salita Lucio Denti 4, Taormina.
Tel: (0942) 23 463.
www.ilpiccologiardino.it

Shalai ★★★

A jewel of a new boutique hotel with spa and creative restaurant. Great atmosphere, nicely designed rooms; perfect as a base for exploring the northeast coast.

Via Guglielmo Marconi 25, Linguaglossa.
Tel: (095) 643 128.
www.shalai.it

Grand Hotel Timeo ★★★★

Stately, beautiful rooms look out over the Gulf of Naxos; restaurant, spa and every service you might expect from the ultimate luxury hotel in Taormina's historic centre.

Greco 59, Taormina.
Tel: (0942) 627 0200.
www.grandhoteltimeo.com

Palmerston Etna Golf Resort & Spa ★★★★

Large full-service resort hotel on Mount Etna with 18-hole golf course, spa and private beach.

Castiglione di Sicilia.
Tel: (0942) 986 384. www.palmerston-etna.com

Central Sicily

Hotel Pomara ★

A surprisingly comfortable, modern, family-run hotel near Armerina and Caltagirone.

Via Veneto 84, San Michele di Ganzaria.
Tel: (0933) 976 976.
www.hotelpomara.com

Resort Mandranova ★★

A resort has been created within the old farm buildings on this olive-oil-producing estate. Find a pleasant atmosphere, lovely rooms and gardens; the restaurant serves well-prepared food. Good base for Agrigento and beaches.

Contrada Mandranova, SS 115 km 217, Palma di Montechiaro.
Tel: (393) 986 2169.
www.mandranova.com

Foresteria Baglio della Luna ★★★

This restored tower stands in the countryside of Agrigento, very near the Valle dei Templi and Agrigento but in tranquil countryside. Good restaurant on site, terrace (and some rooms) with temple views.

Contrada Maddalusa, Valle dei Templi.
Tel: (0922) 511 061.
www.bagliodellaluna.com

Verdura ★★★★

Large, new luxury resort on the south coast with spa facilities and two 18-hole golf courses plus a 9-hole course.

Contrada Verdura, Sciacca.
Tel: (0925) 998 001.
www.verduraresort.com

Southeast Sicily

Dimore del Valentino ★

Self-catering apartments in this sensitively restored stone *masseria* (farmhouse) with

beautiful grounds and pool.
SP 66 Sampieri, Marina di Modica km 1, Scicli. Tel: (0923) 939 751. www. dimoredelvalentino.it

Alla Giudecca ★★
Restored medieval building in the old Jewish ghetto in the very heart of Ortigia.
Via Alagona 52, Siracusa. Tel: (0931) 222 55. www.allagiudecca.it

Monteluce ★★
Farm buildings sited in citrus groves and gardens transformed into luminous apartments; terraces, pool and kitchenettes.
Contrada Vaddeddi, Noto. Tel: (335) 690 1871. www.monteluce.com

Palazzo Failla ★★
The Failla family welcome you into their family palazzo where rooms retain original furnishings. Enjoy La Gazza Ladra, one of Sicily's best restaurants (*see p163*), and there's also a trattoria in the intimate courtyard.
Via Blandini 5, Modica. Tel: (0932) 941 059. www.palazzofailla.it

Talìa ★★
Restored, owned and operated by a pair of architects in full respect for Modican history and tradition. Stone buildings and lush terraces create a tranquil haven with the drama of Modica spread out before your very eyes.

Via Exaudinos 1/9, Modica. Tel: (0932) 752 075. www.casatalia.it

Villa rentals
These are offered by several reliable agencies. **ThinkSicily** is a luxury travel service with the goal of sharing the best of the villas and boutique hotels available in Sicily. Large staff of English and Italians, including staff on the ground in Sicily (*Tel: from the UK (020) 7377 8518; from the USA and Canada (1 800) 490 1107. www.thinksicily.com*).
Cuendet has built a solid reputation over the last 25 years and has a wide selection of villas in Sicily (*www.cuendet.com*).

The tranquil farmhouse Dimore del Valentino, Scicli

Practical guide

Arriving

Entry formalities

A valid passport is all that is needed for most visitors to enter Italy. Visas are not necessary for EU citizens nor for citizens of New Zealand, Australia, Canada and the USA. Your passport allows a stay of 90 days. Those wishing to stay more than 90 days – or to work in Italy – need a permit, available from your home country's consulate or nearest police headquarters.

Arriving by air

From the UK, it is possible to fly direct to Sicily. British Airways flies to Catania, while Ryanair flies straight to Trapani and Palermo. Most other visitors fly to Milan, Naples or Rome, before taking a local flight to one of Sicily's airports. The island's main airport is Aeroporto Falcone e Borsellino, located at Punta Raisi, 31km (19 miles) west of Palermo (trains and bus links to Palermo). Aeroporto Fontanarossa is 7km (4½ miles) south of Catania centre; Vincenzo Florio Airport at Birgi is 20km (12½ miles) south of Trapani; the airport at Comiso, 15km (9 miles) west of Ragusa, awaits permits to open to commercial traffic.

Arriving by boat

There are several ways to get from mainland Italy to Sicily, the most common being the short 12km (7½ miles) hop across the Messina Straits, from Villa San Giovanni in Italy. Reggio di Calabria is another good place from which to catch a *traghetto* (ferry) or, faster still, an *aliscafo* (hydrofoil).

From Naples, there are hydrofoils or ferries to Palermo. Ferries take about ten hours while hydrofoils take half as long (although timings can be affected by adverse weather). GIW and Snav ferries also travel from Genoa, Livorno and Civitavecchia to Palermo, which takes from 12–20 hours.

Arriving by train, car and bus

It is possible to take a train, car or bus to Sicily (via a ferry crossing).

Going by car is the least practical for several reasons. Petrol is relatively expensive here compared to the rest of Europe, and tolls increase motoring costs; the journey from Britain involves many hours behind the wheel.

It is possible to take a bus from a number of cities in Italy: for example, Rome, Pisa, Bologna and Naples. The journey time will be between 9 and 13 hours.

The most practical way of getting to Sicily from the mainland is by train from a large city such as Rome or Naples. The trains reach the port of Villa San Giovanni and then roll on to barges for the one-hour crossing to Messina. Passengers do not have to move from their train seats at all. The whole journey from Rome to Palermo takes around 12 hours.

Camping

Campsites in Sicily vary in standard and in their facilities. Some are little more than a clearing where you can pitch a tent, with very basic toilet and shower facilities; others are much more sophisticated. In general, camping is cheaper than staying in hotels. Independent camping is not allowed. It is advisable to book in advance in high season (June to August).

Climate
Sicily weather chart

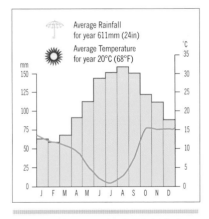

WEATHER CONVERSION
CHART
25.4mm = 1 inch
°F = 1.8 × °C + 32

Crime and safety

The biggest threat is from *scippatori* (purse snatchers), who operate in the big cities such as Palermo and Catania. Be especially careful on popular tourist bus routes such as the bus from Piazza de Indipendenza in Palermo to Monreale Cathedral. Do not walk around deserted streets at night in the big cities; stick to busy streets. Violence is rarely used against tourists.

Car crime is a growing worry in Sicily, with thieves targeting hire cars in particular. Make sure you do not leave anything in your car overnight. Smaller towns and villages are generally much safer than cities.

Customs regulations

In line with other EU countries, Italy allows unlimited amounts of duty-payable goods, as long as the owner is travelling from another EU country and they are for personal use. Guidance levels on goods bought in the EU for your own use are: 800 cigarettes, 200 cigars, 1kg (2.2lb) of smoking tobacco, 10 litres of spirits, 90 litres of wine and 110 litres of beer.

For non-EU citizens, and EU citizens arriving in Italy from non-EU countries,

Town beaches, like this one at Giardini Naxos, can be quite narrow

duty-free limits on duty-payable goods are: 400 cigarettes or a quantity of cigars or pipe tobacco not exceeding 500g (1.1lb). Alcohol limits are 1 litre of spirits and 2 litres of wine. For alcohol bought tax-paid, limits are much more liberal than in other countries of the EU.

For more information, contact:
- Australian Customs Services. *Tel: +061 2 6275 6666. www.customs.gov.au*
- New Zealand Customs. *Tel: 04 473 6099 or 0800 428 786. www.customs.govt.nz*
- Canada Customs and Revenue Agency. *Tel: 800 461 9999 in Canada. www.ccra-adrc.gc.ca*
- US Customs and Border Protection. *Tel: (877) 227 5511. www.cpb.gov*

Driving

Driving around Sicily can be a pleasurable experience, allowing you to travel where you please. However, beware of heavy traffic in the bigger cities. Finding a parking space in cities can be difficult, but car parks are reasonably priced and often offer discounts through your hotel.

Renting a car

To rent a car, you will need to show your driving licence, and an International Driving Permit (IDP) if it is a non-EU licence. You must also have a valid passport, and be more than 25 years old. Insurance on all vehicles is compulsory; any reputable rental firm will be able to arrange this.

It is generally cheaper to arrange car rental before you leave home, although you can of course rent cars once you arrive in Sicily; this can be done most easily at airports.

Road rules

Driving is on the right in Sicily. In cities and towns, the speed limit is 50kmh (31mph); the limit is 90kmh (56mph) on main roads (*strade statali*) and local roads. On the *autostrade* (motorways), the limit is 130kmh (81mph). Use of seat belts is compulsory. Traffic in Italy may appear chaotic; there is, though, a method to the madness. Traffic flows organically. Observe road rules and employ common courtesy and a bit of courage.

Highways and tolls

The system of motorways (*autostrade*) is not extensive in Sicily. The most important road is the A19 between Palermo and Catania. Sicily has nowhere near the number of tolls as mainland Italy. Main roads are known as *strade statali* (state roads), and are mostly single-lane. Out in the country, you may find yourself on dirt roads.

Petrol

The cost of *benzina* (petrol) is very high in Italy. Unleaded petrol is *benzina senza piombo* and diesel is *gasolio*. Petrol stations on the *autostrade* are open 24 hours, but on regular roads they often close from noon to 3pm for lunch, after 7pm at night and all day Sunday. Not all petrol stations offer an after-hours self-service option and when they do, cash is often required.

Breakdowns

The main breakdown service in Sicily is the Automobile Club Italiano (ACI). There is a charge for roadside emergency help. If you call the ACI emergency number (*tel: 116*) in the event of a breakdown, you will be expected to pay a range of charges. Try to make sure your hire car is in good working order before you leave the rental office.

Electricity

The electric current is 50Hz 220V, as in the rest of continental Europe. Plugs have two round prongs or three smaller round prongs. It will be necessary to bring an adaptor plug. It is advisable for visitors to use a transformer when using their own electrical items.

Embassies and consulates

For American and British citizens, there are consulates in Palermo. Office hours are Mon–Fri 9am–3.30pm.
United Kingdom Consulate, Via Cavour 117. Tel: (091) 326 412. Open: Mon, Wed & Fri 9.30am–12.30am.
US Consulate, Via Vaccarini 1.
Tel: (091) 305 857. Open: Mon–Fri 9am–12.30pm.

Embassies are in Rome.
Australian Embassy, Via Alessandria 215. Tel: (06) 85 27 21.

Canadian Embassy, Via G B de Rossi 27. Tel: (06) 85 442 911.
New Zealand Embassy, Via Zara 28. Tel: (06) 853 7501.
UK Embassy, Via XX Settembre 80a. Tel: (06) 42 20 00 01.
USA Embassy, Via Veneto 121. Tel: (06) 467 41.

Emergency telephone numbers

The most important emergency numbers are:
Police *113*
Ambulance *118*
Fire Brigade *115*
Road assistance *116*

In a general crisis, call the *Carabinieri* (military-trained police force) on *112*.

Health

In general, Sicily offers no particular health risks, and vaccinations are not needed. It is easy to get a prescription supplied in towns and cities, and there is usually at least one pharmacy in towns and villages. English-speaking doctors are plentiful at hospitals.

Medical treatment

EU citizens with a European Health Insurance Card (available from *www.ehic.org.uk*, by phoning *0845 606 2030* or from post offices in the UK) are entitled to free emergency treatment. Australia also has a reciprocal agreement run by Medicare. For other nationalities, if you are admitted to a

(*Cont. on p182*)

Language

LANGUAGE

The official language is Italian, but most islanders also speak a Sicilian dialect. This patois is a mix of languages, developed over the centuries and influenced by Sicily's colonisers, having elements of Arabic, Greek, French, English and Spanish. English is often understood at museums, as well as at most hotels and restaurants catering to foreign visitors. Italians appreciate some attempt to speak Italian, even if your prowess only extends to common courtesies such as 'thank you' and 'excuse me'.

Pronunciation

c before a, o and u is hard as in 'cat'
c before e or i is 'ch' as in 'cello'
ch is hard, as in 'kill'
g before a, o and u is hard as in 'go'
gh is also hard
g before e or i is soft, as in 'gin'
gl before e or i is usually pronounced 'lyee', as in 'million'
gn is as the 'ni' in 'onion'
h is always silent
r is a rolled 'rrr' sound
sc before a, o and u is hard as in 'scandal'
sc before e or i is a soft 'sh' as in 'shade'
z is like the 'ts' in 'rats', except at the beginning of a word when it is pronounced as the 'ds' in 'plods'

Basics

Yes – *Sì*
No – *No*
OK! – *Va bene!*
Please – *Per favore/Per piacere*
Don't mention it – *Prego*
Thank you – *Grazie*
Many thanks! – *Grazie mille!*
Cheers (generic toast) – *Salute!*
Mr/Sir (without surname) – *Signor/Signore*
Madam/Mrs – *Signora*
Miss/Ms – *Signorina*
I don't speak Italian – *Non parlo italiano*
I'm sorry... (bad news, or refusing invitation, etc.) – *Mi dispiace...*
I'd like... – *Vorrei...*
I need... – *Ho bisogno di...*
I don't understand – *Non capisco*
Do you understand? – *Lei capisce?*
I don't know – *Non lo so*
Do you speak English? – *Parla inglese?*
Could you repeat that, please? – *Potrebbe ripetere, per favore?*
How much is...? – *Quanto costa...?* (masculine) or *Quanta costa...?* (feminine)

Numbers

1	uno	6	sei
2	due	7	sette
3	tre	8	otto
4	quattro	9	nove
5	cinque	10	dieci

Greetings

Good day/hello (formal) – *Buongiorno*
Hi!/bye! (informal) – *Ciao*
Good evening (after about 3pm) –
  Buona sera
Goodbye – *Arrivederci*
Excuse me/Sorry – *Scusi*
Excuse me (to get by) – *Permesso*
Hello – *Salve*

Accommodation

Is there a hotel here? –
  C'è un albergo qui vicino?
Have you got a room? –
  Avete una camera?
I'd like (to book) a (single/double)
  room... – *Vorrei (prenotare) una*
  camera (singola/doppia)...
with bath – *con bagno*
with shower – *con doccia*
with a double bed –
  con letto matrimoniale
twin-bedded – *a due letti*
with an extra bed for a child –
  con un letto aggiunto per un
  bambino
We'd like to stay...nights –
  Vorremmo restare per...notti
Is breakfast included? –
  La prima colazione è inclusa?
Have you anything cheaper? –
  Avete qualcosa meno caro?
Can you suggest somewhere else? –
  Ci può consigliare un'altro posto?

Eating out

Where can we eat something? –
  Dove possiamo mangiare qualcosa?

not too expensive – *non troppo caro*
Can you recommend a good local
  restaurant? – *Ci può consigliare un*
  buon ristorante locale?
I'd like to book a table for...people –
  Vorrei prenotare un tavolo
  per...persone
for tonight... – *per questa sera...*
for tomorrow night...–
  per domani sera...
at 8 o'clock – *alle otto*
The menu, please –
  Il menù, per favore
What is the dish of the day? –
  Qual è il piatto del giorno?
What is the speciality of the house? –
  Qual è la specialità della casa?
Can you tell me what this is? –
  Mi può spiegare che cos'è questo?
I'll have this – *Prendo questo*
Could we have some more
  bread/more water, please? *Ci dà*
  ancora un po' di pane/un po' di
  acqua, per favore?
The bill, please –
  Il conto, per favore
Is service included? –
  Il servizio è incluso?

osteria – casual restaurant
ristorante – restaurant
trattoria – family-run restaurant
tavola calda – hot snacks
antipasti – starter
primo (piatto) – first course
secondo (piatto) – main course
contorno – vegetables

hospital as an in-patient, even as an accident and an emergency case, you will be required to pay. Most travel insurance policies cover some medical treatment, but be prepared to pay the bills up front at the time of care. Keep all the paperwork so that you can claim the money back when you get home.

Pharmacies

At every pharmacy (*farmacia*) there is a list of those that are open at night and on Sundays. Pharmacies are generally open Mon–Fri 9am–1pm & 4–7pm, and Sat am.

Water

Tap water is safe, while public fountains may or may not be. Unsafe water sources will be marked *acqua non potabile* (non-drinkable water). Most Italians take mineral water with their meals rather than drinking tap water. Bottled mineral water is cheap and available in shops, bars and other outlets. If tap water comes out cloudy, it is usually due to calcium or other minerals inherent in a water supply that often comes untreated from fresh springs.

Insurance

Travel insurance is essential to safeguard against the financial consequences of lost luggage, trip cancellation and receiving emergency medical treatment. Remember to check your existing home insurance policy to see if you already have baggage cover, as you may not need to include this

in your travel insurance. If you do need to make a claim for any reason, ensure that you have any necessary evidence: for example, a police report for stolen items.

Internet

There are Internet cafés in most Sicilian cities and towns; the easiest way to track them down is to check the tourist office or your hotel. Smaller towns and villages are less likely to have these facilities. Wi-Fi coverage is still rare.

Lost property

Remember to take a photocopy of the main sections of your passport, in case you lose the original. If your passport is lost or stolen, head to your consulate as soon as possible for a replacement. To report the loss or theft of personal belongings, go to the nearest police station or find a police officer. A copy of the police report will be necessary to explain your lack of passport and driver's licence and to reclaim the money back from your travel insurance company.

Maps

A highly recommended map is the Touring Club Italiano (TCI) map of Sicily (scale 1:200,000), which is available in airports and appropriate shops. Michelin also produces a map of Sicily, as does GeoCenter International and others. A recommended road atlas is De Agostini's *Atlante Turistico Stradale della Sicilia* (1:250,000).

Media

In major tourist towns, English-language newspapers and magazines are on sale at hotels and news kiosks, but they are hard to find outside major cities.

Money matters

The euro, the single European currency, replaced the Italian lira in 2002. The relative value of the euro fluctuates against the US dollar, the pound sterling and other currencies.

Exchange rates tend to be more favourable at the point of arrival rather than in your home country. However, it is worth exchanging some money before arriving in Sicily, so that you can pay for essentials such as transport from the airport. Banks tend to offer better exchange rates than exchange bureaux, hotels and shops. While credit cards can be used in many places in Sicily, you may find some restaurants and hotels in smaller towns do not accept them.

Many travellers make use of cash-point facilities (ATMs) – called Bancomat – at banks in Sicilian towns, nowadays quite widely seen and available 24 hours a day. You can also draw cash advances at some but not all banks, using your credit card. However, credit-card companies tend to charge high rates of interest for this service. Do not rely on traveller's cheques, which are not easily converted.

National holidays

Offices and shops in Sicily are closed on the following national holidays:

1 January *Anno Nuovo* (New Year's Day)
6 January *Befana* (Epiphany)
Easter Monday *Giorno dopo Pasqua*
25 April *Giorno della Liberazione* (Liberation Day, World War II)
1 May *Giorno del Lavoro* (Labour Day)
15 July *Santa Rosalia*
15 August *Ferragosto* (Assumption of the Virgin)
1 November *Ognissanti* (All Saints' Day)
8 December *Concezione Immaculata* (Feast of the Immaculate Conception)
25 December *Natale* (Christmas Day)
26 December *Festa di Santo Stefano* (St Stephen's Day).

Opening hours

Sicily follows the rest of Italy when it comes to opening hours. The *riposo* (afternoon siesta), when almost everything shuts, remains an important part of Sicilian life. It is a good idea to adopt this tradition as well while in the country, particularly if you are visiting during the summer, when the afternoon sun can be punishing. Normal business hours are 8am or 9am to 1pm, and 3.30 or 4pm to 7pm or 8pm. Some museums, shops and restaurants may have variations on this. Banks usually close at 3pm or 4pm. Sundays are usually extremely quiet in smaller towns, and public transport everywhere will be very limited. The bigger towns are slowly changing, with some businesses remaining open all day and on Sundays.

Organised tours

An escorted tour or special-interest tour can be good value, especially if your time in Sicily is limited. A package including airfare, hotel and transport can often work out cheaper than booking each element separately. The travel sections of some UK Sunday newspapers often have good-value tours advertised. **Italiatour**, a company of the Alitalia Group (*www.italiatours.com*), is one of many offering escorted tours of Sicily. Tourist offices and hotels also have information on organised excursions.

Places of worship

There are a great many churches in Sicilian towns, reflecting the important role that religion still plays in Sicilian life. Most locals attend Mass at least once a week. Churches are usually open from 7am to 7pm or 8pm, some closing between noon and 3pm. Visitors should behave respectfully and courteously and dress conservatively (do not go into churches wearing shorts or with exposed shoulders).

Police

The emergency number for Police is 113. There are several types of police in Sicily. The civil force is the *polizia*, which is controlled by the Ministry of the Interior. Officers wear powder-blue trousers and a navy-blue jacket. They are based at the *questura* (police station). They deal with most tourist-related issues.

The *carabinieri* (military police) are controlled by the Ministry of Defence. They wear dark blue uniforms with a red stripe, and deal with more sensitive issues such as organised crime.

There are also the *polizia municipale* (municipal police), *vigil urbani* (traffic police) and *guardia di finanza*, who are responsible for fighting tax evasion and drug smuggling.

Post offices

You can buy *francobolli* (stamps) at all post offices and *tabacchi* (tobacconists). You can also send items by *posta prioritaria* (priority post), *raccomandata* (registered), *assicurata* (insured) or *posta celere* (urgent mail). Main post offices in the bigger cities are open from 8am to 5pm during the week, and also Saturday mornings. Postal offices in Italy are usually very crowded.

Public transport

Public transport is fairly reliable and very good value compared with other European countries. Buses between cities are very cheap, quite comfortable and the bus network is extensive. Trains are a good idea for longer journeys but are less reliable than buses and the network sparse. In many cases, train stations are located a long way from the town centre.

Air

Internal flights serve Lampedusa in the Pelagie Islands and the island of Pantelleria.

Buses

There is a whole host of bus operators within Sicily, but in general it is fairly straightforward to organise a bus trip. Some cities have more than one bus depot, so it is worth doing some research before your trip. Tourist information offices can help you with timetables and departure points. Buses are the best option for visiting remote villages.

The main bus operator is **SAIS** in Palermo (*tel: (091) 617 1141*) or Catania (*tel: (095) 536 20*). Other operators include **Cuffaro** (*tel: (091) 616 1510*), which serves the area of Agrigento, **Etna Transporti** (*tel: (095) 530 396*), which has routes to central Sicily, and **Interbus** (*tel: (095) 616 7919*), which has a good service to most cities around the island. Try not to travel on a Sunday, as timetables are drastically reduced.

City buses

Tickets for city buses are bought before boarding, and you must validate them once you hop on or you may be fined on the spot. Tickets are generally purchased at ticket booths, tobacconists (*tabacchi*) or newspaper kiosks. Some cities offer a 24-hour transit ticket that can save you money if you plan to use the bus network extensively, going from attraction to attraction. In Palermo, you can obtain a map from bus information kiosks, like the one in Piazza Ruggero Settimo.

The busy harbour at Messina; ferries link with the offshore islands

Trains

Train fares are generally very affordable in Sicily. Trains are operated by Ferrovie dello Stato (FS), the Italian State Railways. For more information, search the website at *www.trenitalia.com* or *Tel: 892021* from anywhere in Italy. If you are planning to travel at the weekend, book early, as trains get crowded. Most cities and towns have a railway station, although some are inconveniently located out of the centre of the town.

Certain trains (the *diretto*, *espresso* and *interegionale*) stop only at the major towns or cities. If you are travelling between major towns or cities, avoid the *regionale* trains (sometimes known as the *locale*), as they stop in every hamlet and take forever.

Pharmacies generally follow standard opening hours

Remember to validate your train ticket at a machine before boarding as you risk a fine if you do not.

Senior citizens

EU senior citizens over the age of 60 qualify for some discounts in Sicily, such as reduced prices of tickets for museums and public transport. Some hotels and airlines also give discounts, so it is worth enquiring to see if that is the case. The 'silver' travel market is expanding too, with some specialist organisations catering specifically to this growing group of tourists. It is worth searching the web for more information.

Sustainable tourism

Thomas Cook is a strong advocate of ethical and fairly traded tourism and believes that the travel experience should be as good for the places visited as it is for the people who visit them. That's why we firmly support The Travel Foundation, a charity that develops solutions to help improve and protect holiday destinations, their environment, traditions and culture. To find out what you can do to make a positive difference to the places you travel to and the people who live there, please visit *www.thetravelfoundation.org.uk*

In addition, in Sicily, for Mafia-free travel contact *www.addiopizzotravel.it*

Taxes

Like other countries in the European Union, Italy imposes a value-added tax, *Imposta di Valore Aggiunto* (IVA), on many goods and services. Non-EU citizens can claim a tax refund if purchases from one retail outlet total at least €180; however, this only applies if the goods are bought in outlets affiliated to the 'Tax-free for tourists' system, which should display stickers in the window. For more information, contact Global Refund Italia (*www.globalrefund.com*).

Taxis

Taxi rates vary from town to town, but in general they are high. In some cities you can ring to order a taxi, but bear in mind that you will pay for the journey from its starting point, not yours. Taxis are not hailed in the street but are available at taxi stands.

Telephones

Despite the widespread use of mobile phones, there are still a gratifying number of orange public pay phones. Some accept only a *carta telefonica* (phone card) or *gettoni* (tokens), which are on sale at *tabacchi* (tobacconists), while others also accept coins.

Phone numbers in Sicily range from four to eight digits, depending on the size of town. To dial direct internationally, dial *00* plus the country code, the area code and the number. The main country codes are:

USA and Canada: *1*

UK: *44*

Ireland: *353*

Australia: *61*

New Zealand: *64*

CONVERSION TABLE

FROM	TO	MULTIPLY BY
Inches	Centimetres	2.54
Feet	Metres	0.3048
Yards	Metres	0.9144
Miles	Kilometres	1.6090
Acres	Hectares	0.4047
Gallons	Litres	4.5460
Ounces	Grams	28.35
Pounds	Grams	453.6
Pounds	Kilograms	0.4536
Tons	Tonnes	1.0160

To convert back, for example from centimetres to inches, divide by the number in the third column.

MEN'S SUITS

UK	36	38	40	42	44	46	48
Italy & Rest of Europe	46	48	50	52	54	56	58
USA	36	38	40	42	44	46	48

DRESS SIZES

UK	8	10	12	14	16	18
France	36	38	40	42	44	46
Italy	38	40	42	44	46	48
Rest of Europe	34	36	38	40	42	44
USA	6	8	10	12	14	16

MEN'S SHIRTS

UK	14	14.5	15	15.5	16	16.5	17
Italy & Rest of Europe	36	37	38	39/40	41	42	43
USA	14	14.5	15	15.5	16	16.5	17

MEN'S SHOES

UK	7	7.5	8.5	9.5	10.5	11
Italy & Rest of Europe	41	42	43	44	45	46
USA	8	8.5	9.5	10.5	11.5	12

WOMEN'S SHOES

UK	4.5	5	5.5	6	6.5	7
Italy & Rest of Europe	38	38	39	39	40	41
USA	7	7.5	8	8.5	9	9.5

To phone Italy from abroad, dial *39* before the area code and number.

Hotels tend to charge high prices for phoning direct, so it is best to make international calls from a public phone or Internet café. The latter in particular are good value and convenient. A recent development is the use of *carte telefoniche internazionali* (international phone cards).

Tel: *1254* for paid national telephone information and listings (in Italian).

Time

Sicily is one hour ahead of Greenwich Mean Time (GMT) and two hours ahead during daylight saving time (which goes into effect in Italy each year from the end of March to the end of September). When it is noon in Sicily, it is 11am in London, 9pm in Sydney, 11pm in Auckland, and 6am in Toronto and New York.

Tipping

In hotels, service charges and tax of 15–19 per cent will automatically be added to a bill. Some restaurants and cafés add a service charge. If you are not sure, ask '*Il servizio è incluso?*' ('Is service included?'). If a service charge has not been added, a tip left on the table is appreciated and will be shared with the other staff. Restaurants must give customers official receipts by law, as must shops, and you must take your receipt, even for small items.

Toilets

Other than at airports, railway stations and tourist sites, public toilets are not very common in Sicily. You can usually

If unsure about leaving a tip, ask '*Il servizio è incluso?*'

use the ones in bars and cafés, though it is a good idea to buy at least a coffee or water in return. You can ask for the toilet by saying, '*Il bagno?*' or '*Dove sono i gabinetti?*'

The toilet signs are very similar for men and women, so be careful! Women's toilets will be marked as *Donne* or *Signore*, men's as *Uomini* or *Signori*.

Tourist information

There are different types of tourist office in Sicily, but on the whole the staff tend to be helpful and knowledgeable, and able to provide maps of the area and details of tourist attractions.

Azienda Autonoma di Soggiorno e Turismo are local tourist boards. They are located in most tourist sites and towns, but vary in quantity of information and quality of service.

Ente Provinciale per il Turismo are provincial tourist boards and can be found in provincial capitals. All provinces are named after their main town.

On the Internet, the Italian State Tourist Board sponsors the site *www.italiantourism.com*, and the Italian State Tourism Board sponsors *www.enit.it*, although they are limited in terms of the information they provide.

For information before you go, contact the **Italian Government Tourist Boards** in the following countries:

Australia: Level 4, 46 Market Street, Sydney, NSW 2000. Tel: (02) 9262 1666.

Canada: 110 Yonge St, Suite 503, Toronto ON M5C IT4. Tel: (416) 925 4882.

United Kingdom: 1 Princes Street, London W1R 8AY. Tel: (020) 7408 1254.

USA: 630 Fifth Avenue, Suite 1565, New York, NY 10111. Tel: (212) 245 5618.

Travellers with disabilities

Italy is not particularly well organised for people with disabilities. Many towns in Sicily have cobblestone streets and very old buildings, which, while somewhat adapted for modern use, have usually not been adapted to an adequate standard for those with disabilities. Wheelchair access to many areas can therefore be difficult. Travellers with disabilities should plan their trip to Sicily carefully, and try to book a tour that can give specialised assistance.

Relevant organisations that can give advice include:

The Royal Association for Disability and Rehabilitation (RADAR), 12 City Forum, 250 City Road, London EC1V 8AF. Tel: (020) 7250 3222.
www.radar.org.uk
The Society for Accessible Travel and Hospitality (SATH), 347 Fifth Avenue, Suite 610, New York, NY 10016, USA. Tel: (212) 447 7284.
www.sath.org

The Italian tourist office in your country will also be able to provide advice on Italian associations for those with disabilities.

Index

Acknowledgements

Thomas Cook Publishing wishes to thank CAROLINE JONES, to whom the copyright belongs, for the photographs in this book, except for the following images:

ALAMY LTD 27
DREAMSTIME.COM 1, 117 (Sabrina Dvihally), 133 (Sergio Bertino), 135 (Fede), 137 (Sebastiano Leggio), 141 (Jakub Parlinec), 155 (Bepsphoto)
THOMAS COOK 11, 93, 177
ELAINE TRIGIANI 5, 32, 42, 51, 71, 78, 81, 128, 157, 164, 166, 175
WIKIMEDIA COMMONS 66 (Dedda 71), 101 (Triquetra)
WORLD PICTURES/PHOTOSHOT 29, 54 (Mauritius images/Volker Mossa), 84, 88, 98, 109, 145, 153, 169, 188

For CAMBRIDGE PUBLISHING MANAGEMENT LTD:
Project editor: Rosalind Munro
Typesetter: Trevor Double
Proofreaders: Cath Senker & Caroline Hunt
Indexer: Marie Lorimer

SEND YOUR THOUGHTS TO
BOOKS@THOMASCOOK.COM

We're committed to providing the very best up-to-date information in our travel guides and constantly strive to make them as useful as they can be. You can help us to improve future editions by letting us have your feedback. If you've made a wonderful discovery on your travels that we don't already feature, if you'd like to inform us about recent changes to anything that we do include, or if you simply want to let us know your thoughts about this guidebook and how we can make it even better – we'd love to hear from you.

Send us ideas, discoveries and recommendations today and then look out for your valuable input in the next edition of this title.

Emails to the above address, or letters to the traveller guides Series Editor, Thomas Cook Publishing, PO Box 227, Coningsby Road, Peterborough PE3 8SB, UK.

Please don't forget to let us know which title your feedback refers to!